# ALGEBRA 1
## ACTIVITIES

**JAMES H. SMITH**

iUniverse, Inc.
Bloomington

**Algebra 1 Activities**

iUniverse books may be ordered through booksellers or by contacting:

iUniverse
1663 Liberty Drive
Bloomington, IN 47403
www.iuniverse.com
1-800-Authors (1-800-288-4677)

ISBN: 978-1-4697-3695-2 (sc)
ISBN: 978-1-4697-3696-9 (e)

Printed in the United States of America

iUniverse rev. date: 10/22/2012

# STAFF CREDITS

## Technical Assistance

Michael Chambers

Vonetta Jackson

Sade' McDowell

Wendell Nicholes

Karl W. Smith

Wayne H. Smith

## Editing

Annie J. Smith

Linda J. Nicholes

Elsie S. Weaver

# About the Author

James Howard Smith received his B.S. degree in mathematics from Norfolk State University in Norfolk, Virginia. Later, he earned a master's degree in Mathematics Education at Old Dominion University in Norfolk, Virginia.

James Smith was a mathematics instructor in the Chesapeake Public School System for thirty-two years. There he taught general mathematics, algebra, and geometry. As an instructor he served on the mathematics textbook selection committee and the mathematics curriculum development committee. Additionally, he participated in several mathematics workshops. He retired from Chesapeake Public Schools in 2000. Since then he has continued to tutor students in all areas of mathematics. Teaching mathematics for many hours at a time has always been a rewarding experience for him. He admits that he truly has a passion for teaching mathematics. This is his reason for writing this algebra activity book.

# Preface

Having served as a high school mathematics instructor for thirty–two years and presently tutoring (middle school, high school, and post graduate students) in algebra, geometry, trigonometry, and calculus, it is my professional opinion that students have a solid foundation in skills crucial to transitioning from simple to complex skills. Students' early mastery of pertinent skills will undoubtedly result in successful mathematics experiences. Therefore, I wrote this book with the instructor and students in mind; that is to facilitate meaningful teaching and learning. Several pages in this book on various mathematics topics may be used as follow-up or supplementary activities following guided instruction based on the instructor's discretion. An abundance of activities is included for extended practice if required. I attempted to arrange them in a sequence which will provide a smooth transfer between mastery of mathematics skills. The instructor may adapt these activities to the students' needs, abilities and learning styles. Hopefully, this book will allow for creativity ,flexibility, and enhancement of learning experiences. Students' thorough mastery of mathematics skills will definitely equip them for careers and challenges of the future.

# Preface

# Table of Contents

# Chapter 1

## Introduction to Algebra

# Verbal Expressions 1

**Directions:** Match the verbal expressions with algebraic expressions by placing the answer on the given line.

| | | | | |
|---|---|---|---|---|
| **1.** | Twice the sum of 6 and A | _____ A. | $2(6+A)$ |
| **2.** | The product of 6 and A increased by 2 | _____ B. | $(A + B) - 6$ |
| **3.** | 6 increased by the sum of A and 2 | _____ C. | $A \div (6 + A)$ |
| **4.** | The quotient of 6 and A plus 2 | _____ D. | $6 - (2 + A)$ |
| **5.** | The difference of 6 and (2+ A) | _____ E. | $(A + B) \div 6$ |
| **6.** | A minus the sum of 6 and A | _____ F. | $6 + (A + 2)$ |
| **7.** | A decreased by the product of 6 and A | _____ G. | $6 \div (A + B)$ |
| **8.** | A divided by the sum of 6 and A | _____ H. | $(6A) + 2$ |
| **9.** | A less than (6 + A) | _____ I. | $6/A + 2$ |
| **10.** | Twice the sum of A and 6 | _____ J. | $A - (6 + A)$ |
| **11.** | Three times the sum of A and 6 | _____ K. | $(A + B) - 6$ |
| **12.** | The product of 6 and B minus A | _____ L. | $2(6 + B)$ |
| **13.** | 6 increased by 6 times 6B | _____ M. | $6 + B$ |
| **14.** | A decreased by 6 times 6B | _____ N. | $2(6+A^2)$ |
| **15.** | The number 6 increased by B | _____ O. | $A - 6(6B)$ |
| **16.** | 6 less than A increased by B | _____ P. | $A - (6A)$ |
| **17.** | Twice the sum of 6 and $A^2$ | _____ Q. | $6 + 6(6B)$ |
| **18.** | 6 divided by the sum of A and B | _____ R. | $(6+A) - A$ |
| **19.** | The sum of A and B divided by 6 | _____ S. | $1/4 A$ |
| **20.** | The sum of A and B decreased by 6 | _____ T. | $2(A + 6)$ |
| **21.** | One fourth of the number A | _____ U. | $3(A + 6)$ |
| **22.** | Twice the sum of 6 and B | _____ V. | $6(B) - A$ |

# Verbal Expressions 2

**Name** _____     **Date** _____

**Directions:** Use one color to shade the correct verbal expression for each algebraic expression. Place the number of the  answer  to each problem in the correct rectangle.

1.  X to the fifth power

2.  The product of 5 and X

3.  Five increased by twice X

4.  One fifth of the square of X

5.  Five times as many wins

6.  Triple the difference of 5 and the cube of X

7.  Five increased by the product of 3 and X

8.  Five increased by X

9.  Five less than X

10.  5 divided by X

11.  5 increased by five times X square

12.  Five minus two times X

13.  Five times four times X

14.  Five times X decreased by X

15.  Five increased by four times X

16.  Five raised to the second power

17.  Negative five times X

18.  The product of three and five times X

19.  X to the fifth power plus X

| | |
|---|---|
| $(X + 5)$ | $5/X$ |
| $-1 \div 2X^2$ | $1 \div 5X^2$ |
| $5X + X$ | $3(5 - X^3)$ |
| $X^5$ | $5 - X^4$ |
| $5$ | $5-X$ |
| $5(4X)$ | $X^4$ |
| $5 + 4X$ | $6 - 3X$ |
| $X^5 + X$ | $5^2$ |
| $3(5X)$ | $-5X$ |
| $5 + 2X$ | $5 - 3X$ |
| $5 - 2X$ | $5 - 2X$ |
| $5 + 3X$ | $5X$ |
| $3X$ | $5 + X$ |
| $X - 5$ | $5 + 5X^2$ |
| $5X - 1$ | $5X - X$ |

# Verbal Expressions 3

**Directions:** Translate each verbal expression to an algebraic expression. Color the answers and place the correct letter in the correct rectangle.

A. Three more than two

B. The product of four and four

C. Two added to five

D. Five times three

E. Five minus four

F. Six plus seven

G. Six divided by three

H. The quotient of three and seven

I. Five less than three

J. Five times two

K. Four divided by five

L. Five less than six

M. Three minus four

N. Eight divided by four

O. Three plus five

P. Six divided by seven

Q. Seven less than eight

R. The difference of six and four

S. Five multiplied by four

T. Five minus three

U. Four more than two

V. The sum of three and five

W. Three more than nine

| 2+3 | 15-1 | 8-4 | 6/3 | 5(4) | 6-5 | 3-4 | 6+7 | 3/7 | 2+3 | 3-5 |
|-----|------|-----|-----|------|-----|-----|-----|-----|-----|-----|
| 6-11 | (4x4) | 8-1 | 4-3 | 5x2 | 4x6 | 5-4 | 15/4 | (6-4) | 5+2 | 1-8 |
| 4/5 | 8/4 | 9+3 | 3+5 | 2+3 | 4/8 | 6/3 | 4+2 | 5-3 | 2/5 | 2+4 |
| (3+5) | 11d | 4/5 | 1+5 | 8-7 | 4(5) | 6/7 | 564 | 1/3 | (3+5) | 5x3 |

Name _____     Date _____

**Directions:** Match each key with the correct algebraic expression.

G     ab/2          D     (a + b)          N     2a + b

H     2a – b        T     ab / b          O     2(a – b)

U     2a            A     a – b           P     a + 2b

I     b – a         F     a – b + a        E     2(a + b)

J     .5ab          K     a / b           L     b + a

**1.)** the sum of a and b _____

**2.)** a increased by twice b _____

**3.)** a decreased by b plus a _____

**4.)** a times b divided by b _____

**5.)** twice the difference of a and b _____

**6.)** a times b divided by two _____

**7.)** twice a decreased by b _____

**8.)** two times the sum of a and b _____

**9.)** a more than b _____

**10.)** a less than b _____

**11.)** twice a increased by b _____

**12.)** twice a _____

**13.)** a minus b _____

**14.)** a divided by b _____

**15.)** one half of ab _____

**16.)** b less than a _____

# Magic Picture 1

Name _____     Date _____

**Directions:** Let a = 230; b = 1004; c= 150; d = 23.5; f = 12.06; g = 2 1/3; h = 3 2/4; i = 2/6.
Solve each problem. Shade the answer in each appropriate box and place the letter in the correct box.

**A.** a + b+c          **B.** a + b + d          **C.** d + c          **D.** b - c          **E.** c - f

**F.** g + h          **G.** h + i          **H.** h - g          **I.** ab          **J.** bc

**K.** da          **L.** gh          **M.** hi          **N.** h/g          **O.** g/h

**P.** i/h          **Q.** ci          **R.** cgh          **S.** (a + b+ c)/10          **T.** c²

**U.** ai          **V.** b - a          **W.** b + a          **X.** i³          **Y.** di

| 173.5 | 1.5 | 1  1/6 | 774 | 8 1/6 | 5 5/6 | 3 5/6 | 1  1/8 |
|-------|-----|--------|-----|-------|-------|-------|--------|
| 2/3 | 3/8 | 24.84 | 854 | 22,500 | 230,920 | 5405 | 7.8  1/3 |
| 2/21 | 1/27 | 1257.5 | 1225 | 1384 | 128.4 | 150600 | 138.4 |
| 50 | 137.94 | 23.84 | 5  4/9 | 173.5 | 1234 | 1  1/6 | 76 2/3 |

# Algebraic Expressions 2

**Name** _____    **Date** _____

**Directions:** Find each person's place on the train by solving the algebraic expressions. Place the letter of each problem in the correct seat on the train. Let: a = 2; b = 3; c = 20; d = 1.1; e = .02; f = 2; h = 1/2; i = 1/2; j = 2 1/2.

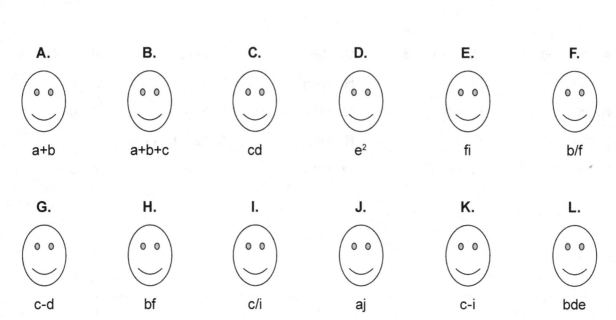

| A. | B. | C. | D. | E. | F. |
|----|----|----|----|----|----|
| a+b | a+b+c | cd | $e^2$ | fi | b/f |

| G. | H. | I. | J. | K. | L. |
|----|----|----|----|----|----|
| c-d | bf | c/i | aj | c-i | bde |

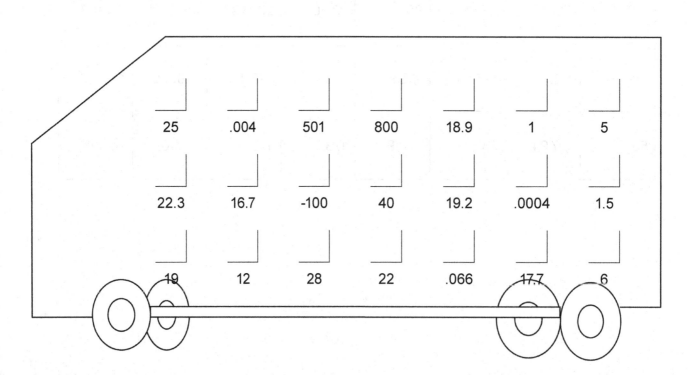

| 25 | .004 | 501 | 800 | 18.9 | 1 | 5 |
|----|------|-----|-----|------|---|---|
| 22.3 | 16.7 | -100 | 40 | 19.2 | .0004 | 1.5 |
| 19 | 12 | 28 | 22 | .066 | 17.7 | 6 |

# Algebraic Expressions 3

**Name** _____  **Date** _____

**Directions:** Find each person's eyes by solving the algebraic expressions. Let a = 2; b = .3; c = 20; d = 1.1; e = .02; f = 20; i = 1/2; and j = -20. Write the letter of the correct answer on each face. Answers are listed below.

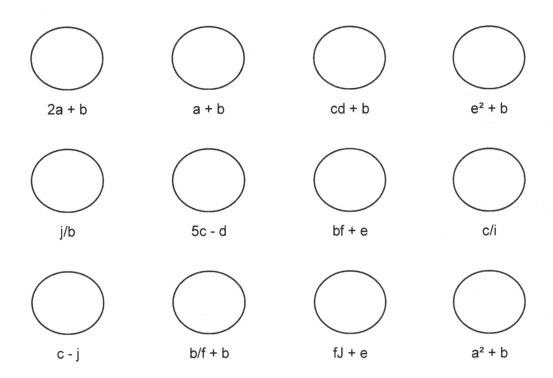

| 2a + b | a + b | cd + b | e² + b |
|--------|-------|--------|--------|

| j/b | 5c - d | bf + e | c/i |
|-----|--------|--------|-----|

| c - j | b/f + b | fJ + e | a² + b |
|-------|---------|--------|--------|

| V(4) | S(5.3) | J(98.9) | W(10.02) | A(22.3) | N(-65.6) |
|------|--------|---------|----------|---------|----------|
| R(89.9) | G(4.3) | O(6.3) | L(4.3) | D(40) | X(.3007) |
| H(41) | M(11.3) | I(22.3) | Q(2.3) | C(.3004) | Z -399.98 |
| B(6.02) | K(.315) | P(.025) | F(10.2) | T(22.1) | E(-66.6) |

9

# Properties of Real Numbers 1

Name _____    Date _____

**Directions:** Place each letter for the correct properties under the correct shapes.

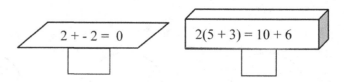

$2 + -2 = 0$

$2(5 + 3) = 10 + 6$

A. Reflexive Property

B. Property of Zero

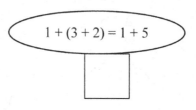

$1 + (3 + 2) = 1 + 5$

C. Additive Identity Property

D. Symmetry Property

E. Distributive Property

$2 \times 1 = 2$

$2 + 1 = 1 + 2$

F. Commutative Property for Multiplication

G. Transitive Property

H. Multiplicative Identity Property

I. Associative Property for Addition

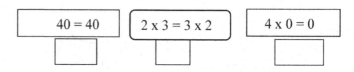

$40 = 40$

$2 \times 3 = 3 \times 2$

$4 \times 0 = 0$

J. Commutative Property for Addition

K. Associative Property for Multiplication

L. Substitution Property

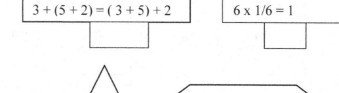

$3 + (5 + 2) = (3 + 5) + 2$

$6 \times 1/6 = 1$

M. Division Rule

N. Additive Inverse Property

O. Multiplicative Inverse

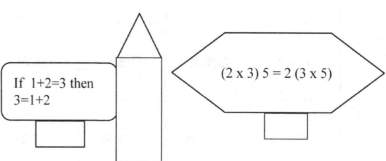

If $1+2=3$ then $3=1+2$

$(2 \times 3)\, 5 = 2\,(3 \times 5)$

# Properties of Real Numbers 2

Name _____     Date _____

**Directions:** Match the properties with the correct definitions by placing the letter in the correct inner circle.

**A.** Reflexive Property

**B.** Property of Zero

**C.** Additive Identity Property

**D.** Symmetry Property

**E.** Distributive Property

**F.** Commutative Property for Multiplication

**G.** Multiplicative Identity Property

**H.** Additive Inverse

**I.** Associative Property for Multiplication

**J.** Commutative Property for Addition

**K.** Associative Property for Addition

**L.** Substitution Property

**M.** Multiplicative Inverse Property

1.  2.  3.  4.

$4 = 4$    $5 + -5 = 0$    $6 + 0 = 6$    $1 + 2 = 2 + 1$

5.  6.  7.  8.

$5 \times 0 = 0$    $6 \times 1 = 6$    $1 \times 2 = 2 \times 1$    $(2 + 3) + 1 = 5 + 1$

9.  10.  11.  12.

$2 \times 1/2 = 1$    $2(X + 3) =$    If $6 = 5 + 1$    $(3 + 2) + 4 =$

$2X + 6$    then    $3 + (2 + 4)$

$5 + 1 = 6$

# Properties of Real Number 3

Name _____     Date _____

**Directions:** Match the properties with the correct shapes by placing the correct letter in the parenthesis.

**A.** Reflexive Property

**B.** Multiplicative Identity

**C.** Associative for Addition

**D.** Distributive Property

**E.** Property of Zero

**F.** Substitution Property

**G.** Symmetry Property

**H.** Transitive Property

**I.** Additive Inverse

**J.** Additive Identity

**K.** Associative for Multiplication

**L.** Multiplicative Inverse

**M.** Commutative for Multiplication

**N.** Property of Zero

**O.** Commutative for Addition

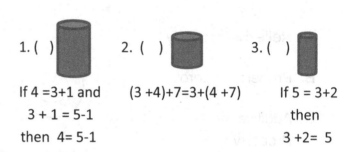

1. ( )     If 4 = 3+1 and
3 + 1 = 5-1
then 4 = 5-1

2. ( )     (3 +4)+7=3+(4 +7)

3. ( )     If 5 = 3+2
then
3 +2 = 5

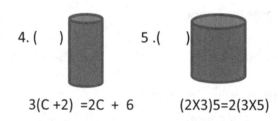

4. ( )     3(C +2) = 2C + 6

5. ( )     (2X3)5 = 2(3X5)

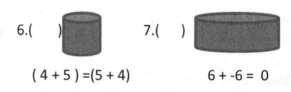

6. ( )     ( 4 + 5 ) = (5 + 4)

7. ( )     6 + -6 = 0

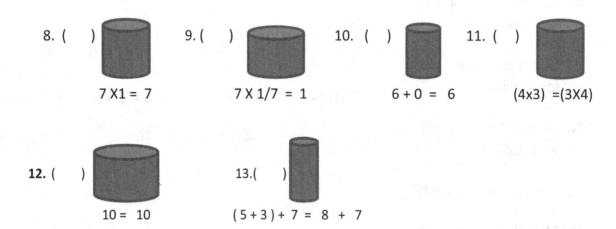

8. ( )     7 X1 = 7

9. ( )     7 X 1/7 = 1

10. ( )     6 + 0 = 6

11. ( )     (4x3) = (3X4)

12. ( )     10 = 10

13. ( )     ( 5 + 3 ) + 7 = 8 + 7

# Properties of Real Numbers 4

**Name** _____     **Date** _____

**Directions:** Name the property for each example.

1.  5 + 0 = 5 _____

2.  6X 1/6 = 1 _____

3.  3X 1 = 3 _____

4.  6X 0 = 0 _____

5.  If 6 = 5 + 1, then 5 + 1 = 6 _____

6.  8 + -8 = 0 _____

7.  If 7 + 3 = 10 + 0 and 10 + 0 = 6 + 4, then 7 + 3 = 6 + 4 _____

8.  6 + (5 + 3) = 6 + 8 _____

9.  6 = 6 _____

10.  3(X + 2) = 3X + 6 _____

11.  (3 + 2) + 7 = 3 + (2 + 7) _____

12.  3 + 7 = 7 + 3 _____

13.  D + 0 = D _____

14.  W x 1 = W _____

15.  A = A _____

16.  G x 0 = 0 _____

17.  4 + (5 + 9) = 4 + 14 _____

18.  W + W = W + W _____

19.  20 x 1 = 20 _____

20.  S (E + 6) = SE + S(6) _____

13

# Properties of Real Numbers 5

Name _____     Date _____

**Directions** If the properties and examples are matched correctly, the time will be correct. Write Yes if the time is correct or No if the time is incorrect.

| 1. Additive Inverse | 2. Additive Identity | 3. Multiplicative Inverse | 4. Property of Zero | 5. Commutative for Addition |
|---|---|---|---|---|
|  |  | | | |
| 8+-8=0 | 6+0=6 | 6X1/6=1 | 6+2=8 | (1+2)+3=1+(2+3) |
| _____ | _____ | _____ | _____ | _____ |

| 6. Distributive Property | 7. Commutative for Multiplication | 8. Associative for Addition | 9. Symmetry Property | 10. Reflexive Property |
|---|---|---|---|---|
|  |  |  |  |  |
| 3(X+2)=3x+6 | 3X2=2X3 | (2X1)3=2X(1X3) | If3=2 and 3=2 them 3=3 | 3=3 |
| _____ | _____ | _____ | _____ | _____ |

| 11. Substitution Property | 12. Transitive Property | 13. Multiplicative Inverse | 14. Commutative for Addition | 15. Additive Identity |
|---|---|---|---|---|
|  |  |  |  |  |
| 3(2+3) = 3(5) | If 3=2+1 and 2+1 =4-1 then 3=4-1 | 6X1/6=1 | 2(3+6)=6+12 | 6+1=7 |
| _____ | _____ | _____ | _____ | _____ |

14

# Chapter 2

Real Numbers

# Adding Integers 1

**Name** _____     **Date** _____

**Directions:** A value for "A" to "Z" is given. Find the sum of each word.

A= -1,      B = -2,      C = -2,      D = -3,      E = 4,      F = -5,      G = 8,      H = -7,

I = 8,      K = -10,     L = 4,       M = -2,      N =-2,      O = 11,     P =-3,      J =-10,

R = -2,     S = 6,       T= -5,       U = 0,       V = -7,     W = 8,      X = -10,    Y = -12,

and Z = -5

1. GOLF _____     2. MY _____

3. TIGER _____     4. BEST _____

5. BASIC _____     6. DIGEST _____

7. RAGE _____     8. TALL _____

9. CITIZEN _____     10. LITTLE _____

11. TRAVEL _____     12. JAMES _____

13. RAYMOND _____     14. PORTABLE _____

15. JACKSON _____     16. AMAZING _____

17. TECHNOLOGY _____     18. ADDING INTEGERS _____

# Adding Integers and Rational Numbers 2

**Name** _____     **Date** _____

**Directions**: Add these integers and place a dot on or near the clock hand.

**1.** 3 + - 7 = _____

**2.** -3 + - 7 = _____

**3.** -1 + -3 _____

**4.** -6 + - 6 = _____

**5.** − 7 + - 3 = _____

**6.** − 6 + - 2 = _____

**7.** 4 + 3 = _____

**8.** -5 + - 4 = _____

**9.** 3 + - 4 = _____

**10.** 6 + - 7 + - 8 = _____

**11.** -1 + -3 + -5 + -2 = _____

**12.** -3 + -4 + 4 + -2 +2 = _____

**13.** 3 + -7 + - 2 + 10 = _____

**14.** -4.6 + - 6.4 = _____

**15.** 5 + 5.8 + 1.2 = _____

**16.** 4 1/3 + 3 2/4 + 1/6 = _____

**17.** 8 + - 4.3 + 3.3 = _____

**18.** -5 2/4 + - 4 1/6 + 2/3 = _____

**19.** 6 3/5 + - 3 2/6 + - 4/15 _____

**20.** 23 + -18 = _____

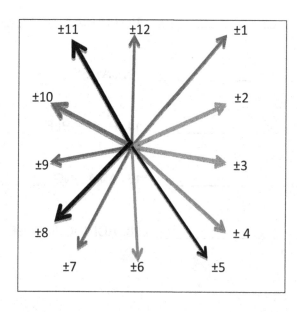

# Adding Integers 3

**Name** _____  **Date** _____

**Directions**: Add these integers.

Open squares are positive.

Closed squares are negative.

In order to add these integers, match the open and closed squares. If you find a match, cross it out. Write the answer that is left.

**1.** Add

1. _____ and _____ = _____

**2.** Add

2. _____ and _____ = _____

**3.** Add

3. _____ and _____ = _____

**4.** Add

4. _____ and _____ = _____

**Study these examples and solve the following problems.**

**5.** 4+6=_____     **6.** 9+-6=_____     **7.** -6+-7=_____     **8.** -6+-4=_____       **9.** -6+-5=_____

**10.** -7+-4=_____     **11.** -5+-3=_____     **12.** 9+-8=_____     **13.** −6+-4+-3+-6=_____     **14.** -7+-5+5+6=_____

**DO YOUR WORK ON THIS PAGE.**

# Adding Integers 4

Name _____   Date _____

**Directions:** Add all integers on the left side and add all integers on the right side. Wizard's team is red and Max's team is green. The team with the largest number of points will win the game.

**WIZARD'S**

| | | | |
|---|---|---|---|
| 18 | -15 | 75 | -76 |
| -86 | 98 | -76 | 65 |
| 34 | -75 | 32 | 97 |
| -7 | -6 | -54 | -56 |
| 87 | -6 | 10 | 43 |

Number of points _____

**MAX'S**

| | | | |
|---|---|---|---|
| -98 | 34 | 76 | -67 |
| 67 | -87 | 76 | -67 |
| 98 | -65 | 87 | -54 |
| -98 | 65 | 98 | -65 |
| -69 | -87 | -98 | -87 |

Number of points _____

**The winner of the game is_____.**

# Adding Integers 5

**Name** _____     **Date** _____

**Directions**: Add the integers on the license plates. Use the values A = -3, B = 2, W=19, C = -5, D = 4, and T = - 6. Place the answers below.

**1.**

> Virginia
> A + B + -3 + -6

**2.**

> New York
> C + D + -9 + 8

**3.**

> Michigan
> C + B + 7 + -7

**4.**

> Minnesota
> B + D + -6 + T

**5.**

> Nevada
> A + -7 + -12

**6.**

> New Jersey
> C + A + -54

**7.**

> Maine
> A + D + B + -64 + T

**8.**

> Maryland
> 8 + A + 54

**9.**

> Iowa
> A + -C + 32 + -45

**10.**

> Illinois
> T + 8 + W + -12

**11.**

> Arizona
> W + B + -76 + 129

**12.**

> Alaska
> 8 + 6 + -64 + -42

1. _____   2. _____   3. _____   4. _____   5. _____   6. _____

7. _____   8. _____   9. _____   10. _____   11. _____   12. _____

# Adding Integers 6

Name _____    Date _____

**Directions:** Add the integers and find two rectangles that have the same answer. Write the letters of the matching rectangles on the lines below.

| | | |
|---|---|---|
| **A**<br>-4 + -9 + 5 + 9 -12 | **B**<br>-6 + -7 + -6 + -6 | **C**<br>-8 + -7 + -5 + -8 |
| **K**<br>10 + 5 + -13+14 | **L**<br>10 + 9 + -6 + 3 | **D**<br>8 + -6 + -13 |
| **F**<br>9 + -5 + 7 + -6 + 2 | **V**<br>6 + 2 + -6 | **R**<br>-2 + -5 + 15 |
| **S**<br>4 + -59 +63 -11 | **Q**<br>-16 + -15 + -11 | **U**<br>-7 + -6 + 9 + -5-19 |
| **N**<br>-2 + 15 + -10 + -6 | **T**<br>-87 + 9 + 15+38 | **E**<br>9 + -4 + -4 + 6 |
| | **J**<br>10 + -1 + -1 | |

1. A & D        2. B & ____        3. C & ____

4. D & ____        5. E & ____        6. F & ____

7. L & ____        8. J & ____        9. N & ____

# Adding Integers 7

Name _____     Date _____

**Directions:** Add these integers.  Find the answers below and shade them.

**1.** 8 + 9 + -6 + 9 = _____

**2.** -3 + 9 + 1 = _____

**3.** 9 + -6 + -5 + -8 + 5 = _____

**4.** -30 + 33 = _____

**5.** -5 + -6 + 22 = _____

**6.** -15 + -10 + 5 = _____

**7.** -8 + -6 = _____

**8.** -30 + 14 = _____

**9.** 53 + -33 = _____

**10.** 16 + 8 + -7 = _____

**11.** 32 +15+-10+14 = _____

**12.** 12 + -6 = _____

**13.** 100 + -15 = _____

**14.** 3 + 7 + -15 + 20 = _____

**15.** -9 + 40 + 4 +20 = _____

**16.** -10 + -9 + -2 = _____

**17.** 12 + -3 = _____

**18.** 40 + 4 +3 = _____

**19.** -15 + -6 + 22 = _____

**20.** 16 + -6 + 6 = _____

**21.** -20 + -4 = _____

**22.** 50 - 9 = _____

**23.** -34 + 27 = _____

| -15 | 1 | 25 | -5 | 21 | 47 | -71 | -19 | 20 |
|-----|-----|-----|-----|-----|-----|-----|-----|-----|
| 22 | 11 | -9 | 39 | 19 | 77 | 41 | 85 | 6 |
| 30 | 51 | 2 | -14 | -20 | 16 | 15 | 20 | 16 |
| -24 | 3 | -16 | 47 | 9 | 11 | -7 | 17 | 7 |
| 55 | 41 | -21 | -24 | -8 | -16 | -8 | 6 | -71 |

# Adding Integers 8

**Name** _____     **Date** _____

**Directions:** Add the given sides of the figures.  Write the sums on the lines.

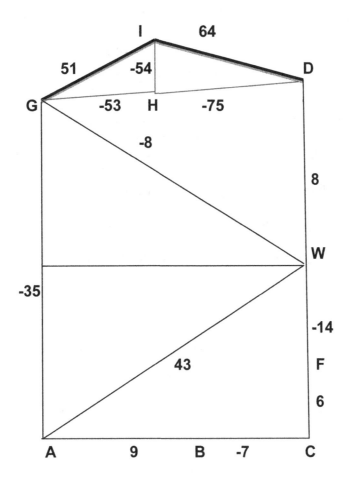

**1.** ABCF _____    **2.** AGHDWA _____    **3.** HDWG _____    **4.** GHDI _____    **5.** GABCW _____

**6.** HDWAB _____    **7.** DWFCA _____    **8.** AWDIG _____    **9.** IHGWA _____    **10.** GHDWA _____

# Adding Integers 9

Name _____ Date _____

**Directions:** Colors are written beside each group of integers. Solve each problem. Find the answers in the pictures below and color them as designated.

**1.** 3 + -7 + 1 = _____ Blue.

**2.** -4 + 6 + -15 + 15 + - 15 = _____ Tan.

**3.** 3 + 30 + -8 = _____ Purple.

**4.** -40 + 16 = _____ Blue.

**5.** 20 + -15 = _____ Red.

**6.** 4 + -4 + -16 = _____ Orange.

**7.** -3 + 10 + -17 + -5 + 35 + 6 = _____ Brown.

**8.** -3 + -7 + -4 + -1 = _____ Blue.

**9.** -6 + -10 + -1 = _____ Pink.

**10.** 8 + 4 + -5 + -7 + 45 = _____ Green.

**11.** -6 + 9 + -14 = _____ Yellow.

**12.** -1 + 1 + 7 + -1 = _____ Gray.

**13.** -18 + -3 + 15 + -8 + 7 = _____ Black.

**14.** -20 + -3 + -10 + 23 = _____ Brown.

**15.** -6 + -2 + -2 + -4 = _____ Green.

**16.** 6 + 8 + -8 + 8 = _____ Yellow.

**17.** 120 + -13 + -21= _____ Red.

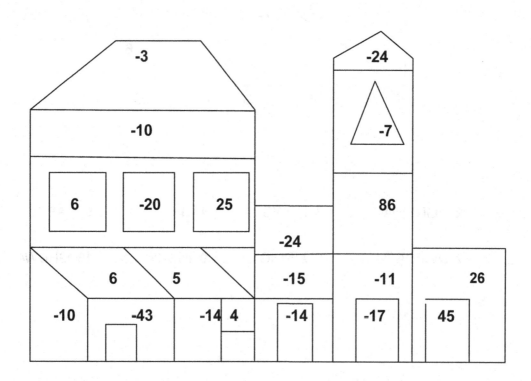

# Adding Integers 10

**Name** _____     **Date** _____

**Directions:** Add these integers and find the answers below. Shade the answers.

**1.** -3 + 9 + -4 = _____     **2.** -7 + -2 = _____     **3.** -3 + -4 + -6 = _____     **4.** 20 + -13+ 4 = _____

**5.** 3 + 4 + 2 = _____     **6.** -11 + 5 = _____     **7.** -2 + -4 + 5 = _____     **8.** -9 + 10 = _____

**9.** -4 + -2 + -5 = _____     **10.** -1 + -2 + 4 + -5 = _____     **11.** 14 + 7 = _____     **12.** 2 8 + -7 + -2 = _____

**13.** -11 + 5 + 6 = _____     **14.** 27 + -19 = _____     **15.** -27 + 11 = _____     **16.** 20 + -27 = _____

**17.** -8 + -10 + 25 = _____     **18.** -3 + -9 + 15 = _____     **19.** 10 + -15 = _____     **20.** 20+-27+-8 = _____

| 2 | -15 | 0 | 3 | 17 | -9 |
|---|---|---|---|---|---|
| 100 | -11 | 13 | 20 | -1 | 34 |
| -7 | 76 | -15 | -6 | 25 | -16 |
| -100 | 21 | 9 | 1 | 11 | -2 |
| 29 | 17 | 18 | -4 | 32 | -5 |
| -13 | 5 | 7 | 63 | 8 | 19 |

# Adding Integers 11

**Name** _____    **Date** _____

**Directions:** Find the total number of boxes in each group. What is the total number boxes in all groups?

Group A

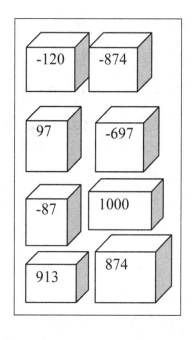

Group B

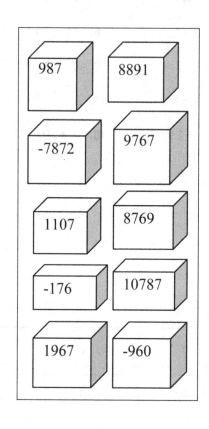

_____                    _____

**Total = _____**

# Adding Integers 12

**Name** _____     **Date** _____

**Directions:** Add these integers horizontally and vertically to find the same answer. Find the total number of days. Check "March" problem to determine if the problems are correct. Answer Yes or No?

## JANUARY

| S | M | T | W | Th | F | Answers |
|---|---|---|---|---|---|---------|
| 2 | -4 | -1 | -5 | 32 | -53 | |
| -4 | 9 | 4 | -7 | -42 | -5 | |
| -3 | -3 | -5 | -5 | 0 | 32 | |
| | | | | | | |

## February

| S | M | T | W | Th | F | Answers |
|---|---|---|---|---|---|---------|
| 2 | -4 | -1 | -5 | 32 | -53 | |
| -4 | 9 | 4 | -7 | -43 | -5 | |
| -3 | -3 | -5 | -6 | -54 | -6 | |
| | | | | | | |

## March     Yes or No _____

| S | M | T | W | Th | F | Answers |
|---|---|---|---|---|---|---------|
| -453 | 543 | -654 | -453 | 876 | 769 | 628 |
| 876 | -654 | -654 | 876 | -876 | 987 | 555 |
| -123 | -124 | -134 | 124 | 124 | 123 | 235 |
| 300 | -235 | -1442 | 547 | 124 | 1879 | 1418 |

# Adding Integers and Rational Numbers 1

**Name** _____     **Date** _____

**Directions:** Add integers and rational numbers by following the codes below.

A

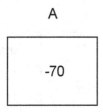

-70

B

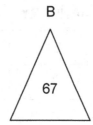

67

C

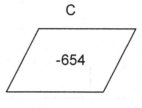

-654

D

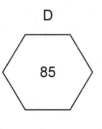

85

E

23.77

F

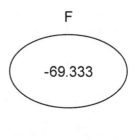

-69.333

G

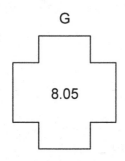

8.05

H

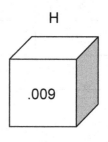

.009

**1.** Add all ADCEF     **2.** Add all ABCH     **3.** Add all ABCGH     **4.** Add all ADGF

_____     _____     _____     _____

**5.** Add all DFH     **6.** Add all BFGE     **7.** Add all AEF     **8.** Add all BGF

_____     _____     _____     _____

# Subtracting Integers 1

Name _____     Date _____

**Directions**: Subtract these integers. Place the answers under each problem. Use red for examples 1 – 10. Use yellow for examples 11 – 15. Use green for examples 16 – 20. Color the answers in the given boxes.

**1.** 4 - ( 5 )        **2.** 14 - ( 14 )        **3.** 6 - ( 7 )        **4.** 2 - ( - 61 )

**5.** 5 - ( 21 )        **6.** - 8 - ( 8 )        **7.** 2 – ( -54 )        **8.** 7 - ( - 7 )

**9.** – 6 - ( - 10 )        **10.** 8 - ( - 7 )        **11.** 6 - ( 3 )        **12.** 14 - ( - 14 )

**13.** – 3 – ( - 7 )        **14.** 2 - ( - 2 )        **15.** 20 - ( - 7 )        **16.** - 3 - ( 7 )

**17.** 9 - ( - 8 )        **18.** 8 - ( 7 )        **19.** 7 - ( 0 )        **20.** 1 - ( - 7 )

| 63 | 15 | 56 | 3 | -16 | 0 | 8 | 4 | 1 | -16 | 13 | - 28 | -97 |
|----|----|----|----|----|----|----|----|----|----|----|----|----|
| 4 | - 10 | 14 | 17 | 27 | 16 | 1 | -1 | 7 | - 13 | 28 | 16 | 4 |

# Subtracting Integers 2

Name _____   Date _____

**Directions**: Find the amount of gasoline in each tank by using subtraction. Write the answer in the lower part of the tank.

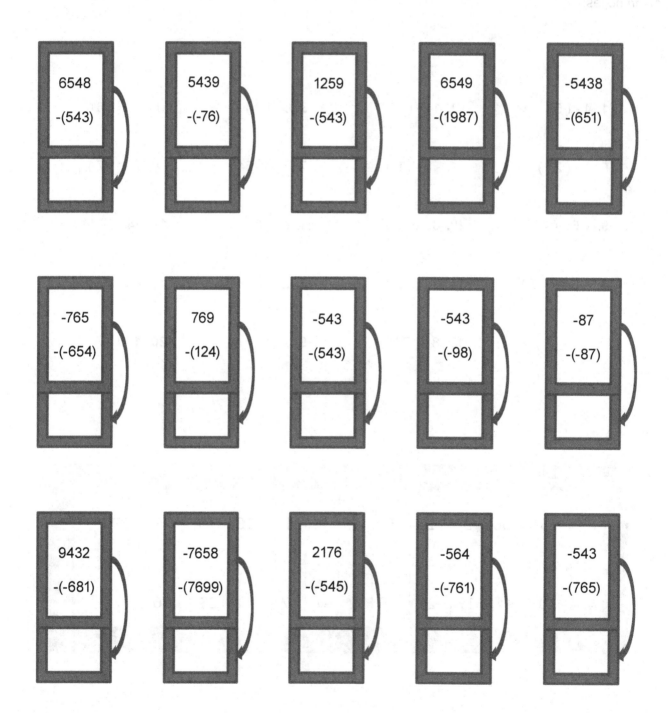

6548
-(543)

5439
-(-76)

1259
-(543)

6549
-(1987)

-5438
-(651)

-765
-(-654)

769
-(124)

-543
-(543)

-543
-(-98)

-87
-(-87)

9432
-(-681)

-7658
-(7699)

2176
-(-545)

-564
-(-761)

-543
-(765)

# Subtracting Integers 3

**Name** _____   **Date** _____

**Directions**: Subtract these integers to determine if the answers are correct or incorrect. Use red crayon to shade yes( Y ) and yellow to shade no(N).

**1.** 8 - ( - 7 ) = 15          **2.** 8 - ( 7 ) = -1          **3.** - 8 - ( - 3 ) = 10

**4.** 7 - ( - 3 )= 10          **5.** - 3 - ( - 2 ) = - 1          **6.** - 3 - ( - 8 ) = 5

**7.** - 3 - ( - 4 ) = 1          **8.** 3 - ( - 5 ) = 8          **9.** 3 - ( - 5 ) = 3

**10.** 12 - ( 7 ) = -19          **11.** 12 - ( - 7 ) = 19          **12.** 12 - ( - 7 ) = 19.

**13.** - 12 - ( - 10 ) = 22          **14.** - 8 - ( - 8 ) = 0          **15.** - 8 - ( 8 ) = - 16.

**16.** - 8 - ( - 7) = 1          **17.** - 9 - ( 7 ) = 2          **18.** - 4 - ( 7 ) - ( - 9 ) - ( - 3)- ( 3 ) = 6

| 1. | 2. | 3. | 4. | 5. | 6. |
|----|----|----|----|----|----|
|  |  |  |  |  |  |

| 7. | 8. | 9. | 10. | 11. | 12. |
|----|----|----|----|-----|-----|
|  |  |  |  |  |  |

| 13. | 14. | 15. | 16. | 17. | 18. |
|-----|-----|-----|-----|-----|-----|
|  |  |  |  |  |  |

# Subtracting Integers 4

Name _____     Date _____

**Directions**: Solve the equations in the boxes below. Find the correct ring sizes that match the equations. Write the letter of the ring beside the numerals.

A = ( 94 )     B = ( 127 )     C = ( - 47 )     D = ( 104 )

E = ( - 54 )     F = ( 108 )     G = ( - 177 )     H = ( 91 )

I = ( 43 )     L = ( - 43 )     K = ( - 82 )     N = ( - 51 )

| 1. | 2. | 3. | 4. | 5. | 6. | 7. |
|----|----|----|----|----|----|----|
| H - L | B - D | K - F | N - A | G - B | D - F | H - N |

| 8. | 9. | 10. | 11. | 12. | 13. | 14. |
|----|----|----|----|----|----|----|
| L - D | A - N | H - F | A - C | D - A | C - F | B - K |

34

# Subtracting Integers 5

**Name** _____     **Date** _____

**Directions**: Imagine you are driving your car by following the arrows. Subtract integers as you drive. As you drive write your answers in the small boxes. Where do you stop ? You may change this number to get many different answers at the end.

Begin.

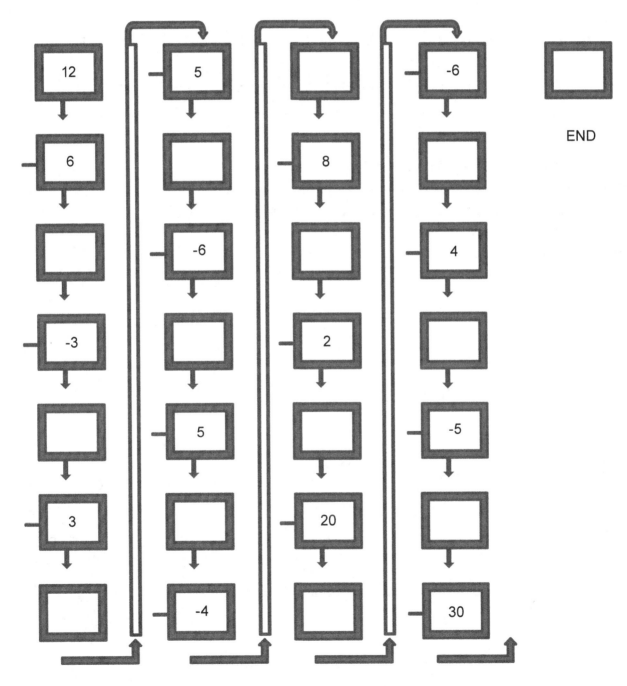

# Subtracting Integers 6

**Directions**: Subtract these integers . A = 3, B = 4, C = - 3, D = - 5, E = 8, F = - 4, and G = - 10.

| | | | | |
|---|---|---|---|---|
| **1.** A - B | **2.** B - C | **3.** C - D | **4.** D - E | **5.** E - F |
| **6.** F - G | **7.** G - A | **8.** G - C | **9.** G - D | **10.** G - G |
| **11.** G - F | **12.** G - B | **13.** C - A | **14.** E - G | **15.** D - F |
| **16.** F - A | **17.** F - B + 2 | **18.** F - B | **19.** E - B | **20.** G - B |

When you solve each subtraction problem, red = 1, green = - 1,
yellow = 12, blue = 0, green = - 18, brown = - 13, pink = 18, orange = 6
red = 20, blue = 0, orange = - 6, red = 14, black = - 5, yellow = 6, tan = - 7,
green = 8, pink = - 8, black = 6, gray = 2,
brown = - 14, and tan = 7

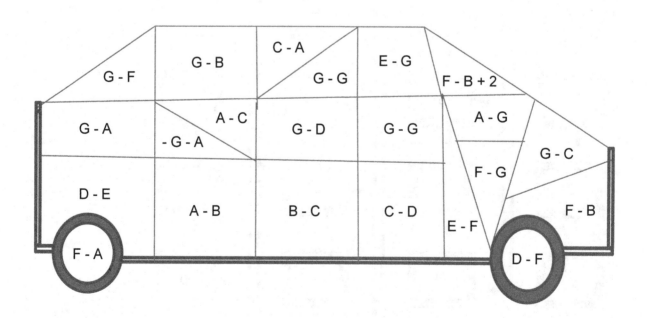

# Subtracting Integers and Rational Numbers 7

Name _____  Date _____

**Directions**: Find the difference between the pairs of objects below.

A.  $ 7.53   B.  $ 18.37   C.  $ - 9.38   D.  $ - 9.84   E.  $ 39.07

F.  $ .06   G.  $ - 5.18   H.  $ - 120.87   I.  $ 30.71   J.  $ - 22.74

L.  $ 57.31   M.  $ - 3.30   N.  $ 98   O.  $ 18.01   P.  $ 9.75

| 1. | 2. | 3. | 4. | 5. | 6. |
|---|---|---|---|---|---|
| B - A | C - D | E - F | G - 1 | H - P | N - H |

| 7. | 8. | 9. | 10. | 11. | 12. |
|---|---|---|---|---|---|
| O - M | L - D | J - B | A - L | F - G | O - D |

| 13. | 14. | 15. | 16. | 17. | 18. |
|---|---|---|---|---|---|
| N - B | M - F | E - F | P - C | G - B | H - E |

# Multiplying Integers 1

**Name** _____     **Date** _____

**Directions:** Multiply the integers and connect the answers to discover the hidden picture.

**1.** -2 x -2 x -2 x 2 = _____      **2.** -1 x -2 x -3 x 2 x -1 = _____      **3.** -3 x -3 x -3 = _____

**4.** -1 x -1 x -4 x -1 = _____      **5.** -1 x -1 x 6 x 4 = _____      **6.** -7 x -4 = _____

**7.** 3 x 9 = _____      **8.** -3 x -9 x -2 = _____      **9.** -3 x -1 x -2 = _____

**10.** 2 x -2 x -10 = _____      **11.** 17 x -2 = _____      **12.** -11 x -2 = _____

**13.** 100 x 0 x 2 x -5 = _____      **14.** -8 x -2 x 2 = _____      **15.** -1 x -75 = _____

**16.** -2 x 2 x 2 x 3 = _____      **17.** 2 x 3 x -2 = _____      **18.** 5 x 5 x -1 x -1= _____

**19.** -9 x 9 = _____      **20.** -1 x 2 x 3 x 1 x 5 x -1 = _____      **21.** 9 x 8 = _____

**22.** 8 x - 2 x 1= _____

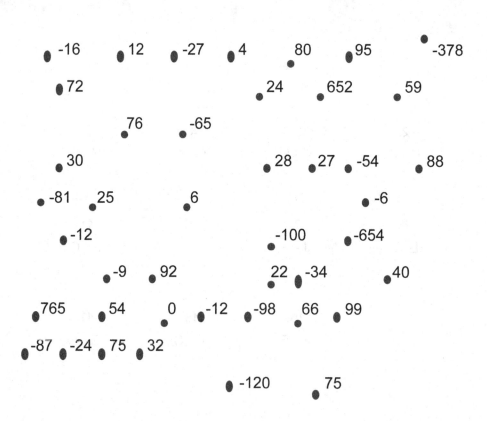

38

# Multiplying Integers 2

Name _____    Date _____

**Directions:** Multiply these integers. Locate the answers in the boxes below. Write the number of the example in the corner of the box containing the answer. Use red for examples 1 to 6. Use yellow for examples 7 to 12. Use blue for examples 13 to 18.

**1.** 2 x 2 x -3 x -4 = _____    **2.** -3 x -2 x -5 = _____    **3.** 2 x 3 x 2 x 1 x 2 = _____

**4.** 1 x -2 x -3 x -2 = _____    **5.** -2 x -1 x -7 x -3 = _____    **6.** 1 x -2 x -3 x -10 = _____

**7.** -3 x 2 x 8 x -3 = _____    **8.** -1 x 2 x 2 = _____    **9.** 100 x 4 x 0 x 765 = _____

**10.** -1 x 1 x -1 x 3 = _____    **11.** -1 x -4 x -3 x -2 x 5 x -2 =_____    **12.** -2 x 4 = _____

**13.** -8 x 2 = _____    **14.** -17 x -1 x -2 x -1 = _____    **15.** 7 x -1 x -1 x 2 = _____

**16.** 11 x -11 x 1 = _____    **17.** -3 x 7 x 3 X-2 x -5 = _____    **18.** 3 x 7 x -3 x -2 = _____

| 48 | 14 | -44 | -8 | -121 | -20 | -12 |
|----|----|-----|----|------|-----|-----|
| 56 | 100 | -30 | 3 | 24 | -240 | -16 |
| 42 | 48 | -630 | -543 | 34 | 126 | 0 |
| 98 | -60 | -10 | 144 | -654 | -4 | -78 |

# Multiplying Integers and Rational Numbers 3

Name _____     Date _____

**Directions:** Multiply the integers on the right. Match the correct person's name beside each state. Some names may not have a match.

Virginia (27) _____     **1.** Jack    2 x 2 x 1 x 2 x 2 = ____

Maryland (-8) _____     **2.** Bill    -2 x -2 x -2 x 1 = ____

California (60) _____     **3.** Mary    -2 x -2 x -1 x -1 x 6 = ____

Colorado (-27) _____     **4.** Bob    -1 x -1 x -1 x -1 x -1 x -32 = ____

Hawaii (-20) _____     **5.** Jerry    3 x -7 = ____

Texas (0) _____     **6.** Tom    -6 x -7 = ____

Illinois (16) _____     **7.** Alt    -3 x -3 x -3 = ____

Indiana (-42) _____     **8.** Jan    100 x 7 x 1 = ____

Kansas (-32) _____     **9.** Bird    -3 x 0 x -2 = ____

Michigan (24) _____     **10.** Tim    5 x 1 x -1 x -2 = ____

Ohio (-21) _____     **11.** Jim    -4 x -2 x -2 x 2 = ____

Wisconsin (-9) _____     **12.** Will    -3 x -3 x 3 = ____

Maine (32) _____     **13.** Ted    2 x -2 x -3 x -1 x 1/2 = ____

Connecticut (-6) _____     **14.** Bull    5 x 5 x 5 x 5 = ____

New York (42) _____     **15.** Todd    -2 x -2 x -3 x -1 x 1/2 = ____

Rhode Island (625) _____     **16.** Can    2 x -3 x -7 x -1 = ____

North Carolina (10) _____     **17.** Shell    3 x -1 x -2 x 10 = ____

Georgia (700) _____     **18.** Paul    2 x -10 = ____

40

# Multiplying Integers 4

Name _____     Date _____

**Directions:** Multiply the integers. Find the letter that goes with each problem. Write the letter beside each problem.

**1.** 2 x 3 = _____

**2.** -2 x -2 = _____

**3.** 2 x - 2 = _____

**4.** 4 x -2 = _____

**5.** -4 x 3 = _____

**6.** -6 x 0 = _____

**7.** 10 x 7 = _____

**8.** -3 x -2 x 2 = _____

**9.** -2 x -3 x -1 x 3 = _____

**10.** -2 x -3 x1 x 3 = _____

**11.** -2 x 3 x -5 = _____

**12.** 2 x 3 x -5 = _____

**13.** 1 x -2 = _____

**14.** -1 x -3 = _____

**15.** -1 x -3 x -2 = _____

**16.** 2 x 2 x 2 x -2 = _____

**17.** 4 x -2 x -2 = _____

**18.** -3 x 4 x -4 x-3 = _____

**19.** 3 x -4 x -2 x 6 = _____

**20.** -3 x -3 x -2 x -1 = _____

**21.** 1 x -3 x -2 x -2 = _____

**22.** 3 x -3 x -2 x -2 = _____

**23.** 9 x 3 x 7 x -2 = _____

**24.** -9 x 2 x 7 x -2 = _____

**25.** 9x6x-1 x 2 = _____

**26.** 3 x -3 x -4 x -2 = _____

**27.** -2 x 9 x 4 x -3 = _____

**28.** -2 x -2 x -2 x -4 x -2 = _____

**29.** -2 x 9 x 3 x -3 x -2 = _____

| 40 | 6 | -36 | 4 | -4 | -6 | 18 | -2 | -8 |
|----|----|-----|----|----|----|----|----|----|
| A | B | C | D | E | F | G | H | I |

| -144 | -12 | 144 | 0 | 16 | 3 | -18 | -30 | 30 |
|------|-----|-----|----|----|----|-----|-----|-----|
| J | K | L | M | N | O | P | Q | R |

| 70 | -16 | 12 | 252 | 216 | -72 | 324 | -378 | -64 |
|----|-----|----|-----|-----|-----|-----|------|-----|
| S | T | U | V | W | X | Y | Z | $A_1$ |

| -108 |
|------|
| $B_1$ |

41

# Multiplying Integers 5

**Name** _____     **Date** _____

**Directions**: Use scissors to cut out the given rectangles. The game is played similar to dominoes. Connect the second rectangle with each given rectangle.

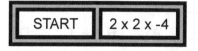

| | START | 2 x 2 x -4 |
|---|---|---|

| | | | |
|---|---|---|---|
| 200 | 7 x 7 x -2 | -16 | 11 x 11 |
| 0 | -4 x -10 | 100 | 2 x 2 x 5 x 2 x 5 |
| 64 | -2x2x-2 X-1X2 | 72 | 2 x 2 x 5 x 3 x 3 |
| 40 | -2 x 2 x 2 x 2 | 121 | -1 x -1 x -9 |
| 48 | 2 x 5 x 2 x 5 | 256 | 2 x 2 x 2 x 3 x 3 |
| -6 | 0 x 2 x 3 x 45 | -16 | -5 x -3 x 2 |
| 192 | 2 x 2 x 2 x 2 x 2 x 2 x 2 x 2 | -9 | 7 x -2 |
| 180 | 3 x 2 x 2 x 2 x 2 | -32 | -1 x 2 x -3 x 2 x -1 x 7 |
| -14 | 2 x 2 x 2 x 2 x 2 x 2 | -84 | 1 x -1 x -2 x -3 x -1 x -1 |
| -98 | End | 30 | 2 x 2 x 2 x 2 x 2 x 2 x 3 |

# Multiplying Integers 6

Name _____     Date _____

**Directions:** Multiply these numbers and place the letters above the answers on the number line.

**A.** 2 x 8 x -2 x 1 = _____

**B.** 1 x -3 x -2 x 32 = _____

**C.** -2 x -1 x 24 x 3 x 1 = _____

**D.** -2 x -1 x -1 x 23 = _____

**E.** 22 x -3 x -2 x -1 = _____

**F.** -1 x -16 x -2 x -2 x -1 = _____

**G.** 1 x 3 x 1 x 36 x 1 = _____

**H.** 46 x 1 x -2 x -2 = _____

**I.** 2 x 38 x -2 x -1 x 1 = _____

**J.** -1 x -2 x 43 x 1 = _____

**K.** 1 x -2 x 47 x -2 = _____

**L.** 2 x 54 x -2 x 0 = _____

**M.** 1 x 75 x -1 x 2 = _____

**N.** 48 x -3 x -1 x 1 = _____

**O.** 1 x 87X -1 x -1 x 2 = _____

**P.** -3 x 29 x -2 = _____

**Q.** 1 x 65 x -1 x -3 = _____

**R.** 1 x -35 X 2X 2= _____

```
0   10  20  30  40  50  60  70  80  90  100 110 120 130 140 150 160 170 180 190 200 210
```

```
-200 -190 -180 -170 -160 -150 -140 -130 -120 -110 -100 -90  -80  -70  -60  -50  -40  -30  -20  -10   0
```

43

# Multiplying Integers 7

**Directions:** Find the product of these integers. Then circle the answers in the box below. Some answers are not given in the box.

**1.** 2 x -3 x -2 = _____

**2.** -2 x -2 x -6 = _____

**3.** -1 x -1 x -1 x -1 = _____

**4.** -3 x 3 x -3 = _____

**5.** -2 x -2 x -2 x -2 x -2 = _____

**6.** 10 x – 14 = _____

**7.** -2 x 2 x -2 x 2 x -2 x 2 = _____

**8.** -3 x 2 x -2 = _____

**9.** -6 x -7 = _____

**10.** -3 x 2 x -2 x -3 =_____

**11.** 5 x 4 x -1 x -2 = _____

**12.** 3 x 2 = _____

**13.** -4 x -2 x -3 = _____

**14.** -8 x -8 = _____

**15.** 5 x -3 x 2 = _____

**16.** -3 x -10 = _____

**17.** 2 x 4 x 3 = _____

**18.** 3 x -6 x 0 = _____

**19.** -3 x -2 x 2 = _____

**20.** -3 x -4 = _____

| 4 | -32 | 30 | 94 | -81 | 1 |
|---|---|---|---|---|---|
| 40 | 42 | 24 | 34 | -101 | 7 |
| 7 | 64 | -36 | 68 | -63 | 36 |
| 3 | 47 | -1 | -120 | 0 | 120 |
| -3 | 32 | -24 | -30 | 101 | -47 |
| 12 | 27 | 140 | -140 | -64 | -30 |

# Multiplying and Dividing Rational Numbers 8

**Name** _____     **Date** _____

**Directions**: Write the name of each item that can be purchased on the correct line. Some items cannot be purchased.

1.  (-2) ÷ 6 _____

2.  -9 1/3 X -3 3/4 _____

3.  5/8 X 4/5 _____

4.  1 /2 ÷ 5/8 _____

5.  -2 1 /2 ÷ -1 _____

6.  -6 X 7/12 _____

7.  2 1 /2 X 3 1/5 _____

8.  2 3 /4 ÷ -4 _____

9.  3 1/3 X 0 _____

10.  -6 ÷ 4/2 _____

11.  -1/3 X 6/-3 X 2/3 X -3/8 _____

12.  -3 1 / 4 ÷ 2 _____

13.  3 4/8 X 1 7/8 _____

14.  6 3 /4 X 3 2/6 _____

15.  2 1 /2 ÷ 1 7/8 _____

16.  -3 ÷ 1 /2 _____

| **Cup** | **Ring** | **Boat** |
|---|---|---|
| -3 ½ | 1 ⅓ | -6 |

| **Glass** | **Box** | **Ball** |
|---|---|---|
| 8 | -11/16 | ½ |

| **Cylinder** | **Watch** | **Hat** |
|---|---|---|
| 6 9/16 | 22 ½ | -3 |

| **Cube** | **Cone** | **Pen** |
|---|---|---|
| 2/5 | 0 | -1 ⅝ |

# Multiplying Integers and Rational Numbers 9

Name _____     Date _____

**Directions:** Select the following letter combinations and find the product. Show each step.

| | | | | | |
|---|---|---|---|---|---|
| **1.** AB | **2.** BC | **3.** CD | **4.** DE | **5.** EF | **6.** FG |
| **7.** GH | **8.** HI | **9.** IJ | **10.** JC | **11.** DE | **12.** AK |
| **13.** IE | **14.** AF | **15.** FK | **16.** AH | **17.** AI | **18.** CI |
| **19.** BD | **20.** FE | **21.** BF | **22.** BG | **23.** BH | **24.** BI |

| 3 | -3 | -5 ⅔ | 4 ⅓ | -2 ⅔ | -⅓ | -3 | -1 | -¾ | 9 | 1 ½ |
|---|---|---|---|---|---|---|---|---|---|---|
| A | B | C | D | E | F | G | H | I | J | K |

| | | | |
|---|---|---|---|
| **1.** | **2.** | **3.** | **4.** |
| **5.** | **6.** | **7.** | **8.** |
| **9.** | **10.** | **11.** | **12.** |
| **13.** | **14.** | **15.** | **16.** |
| **17.** | **18.** | **19.** | **20.** |
| **21.** | **22.** | **23.** | **24.** |

# Multiplying Integers and Rational Numbers 10

**Name** _____   **Date** _____

**Directions:** Multiply the integers and rational numbers in the boxes. Place the answers on the lines below.

**1.**

| | | | | | |
|---|---|---|---|---|---|
| -1 | -1 | -1 | -2 | -2 | -2 |
| -7 | | | | | -1/2 |
| -1 | -1 | -2 | -1 | -2 | -1 |

**2.**

| | | | |
|---|---|---|---|
| -4 | -5 | -8 | +54 |
| -3 | | | - 6 |
| -1 -1 | -2 -1 | -2 | -1 |

**3.**

| | | | |
|---|---|---|---|
| -11 | -2 | -3 | -1 |
| -2 | | | +1/2 |
| -2 | +1+ 2 | -2 | -1 |

**4.**

| | | | | |
|---|---|---|---|---|
| -1 | -1 | -1 | -1 | -2 |
| -1 | | | | -2 |
| -2 | -1 | -2 | +1 | -3 |

**5.**

| | | |
|---|---|---|
| +2 1/6 | | +4 1/2 |
| +3 | | -2 |
| +1/2 | -3 | -1 1/2 |

**6.**

| | | |
|---|---|---|
| -1½ | +6 | +1 |
| +3 | | +1 |
| -7 -1 | +1/2 | +2 |

**7.**

| | | |
|---|---|---|
| 0 | +2 | +345 |
| +6 | | +7 |
| +8 +9 | +10 +1 | +2 |

**Find the product of the seven rectangles.**

1. _____   2. _____   3. _____   4. _____   5. _____   6. _____   7. _____

# Dividing Integers and Rational Numbers 1

Name _____     Date _____

**Directions:** Solve each problem and connect each answer to form a picture.

1. 6 ÷ - 1/6 = _____          2. 6 ÷ 1/6 = _____          3. -6 ÷ -6 = _____          4. 6 ÷ -6 = _____

5. 12 ÷ 6 = _____          6. 12 ÷-6 = _____          7. -12 ÷ -6 = _____          8. -12 ÷ 6 = _____

9. 3 ÷ 3 = _____          10. 3 ÷ -3 = _____          11. 2 1/2 ÷ 2 = _____          12. 3/2÷ -3/2 = _____

13. 3/2 ÷ 1/2 = _____          14. 12 ÷ 6 = _____          15. -12 ÷ 1/3 = _____          16. 8 ÷ 1/2 = _____

17. 8 ÷ -1/2 = _____          18. 0/6 = _____          19. 4 ÷ -2 = _____          20. 6 ÷ -1/3 = _____

21. 6 ÷ -1/6 = _____

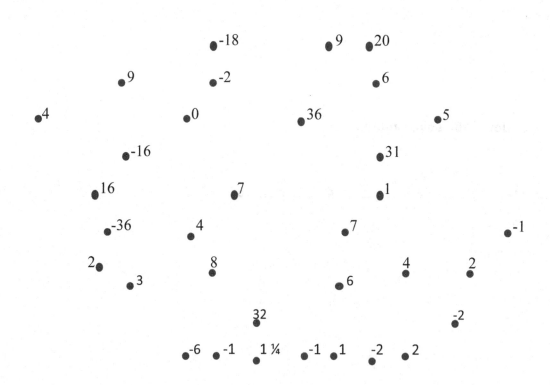

48

# Dividing Integers and Rational Numbers 2

Name _____   Date _____

**Directions**: Solve each problem. Write the letter of the correct answer found in each box below on the correct line by each numeral.

**1.** 8 ÷ 4

**2.** 4 ÷ 8

**3.** 2/6 ÷ 4

**4.** 2 / 3 ÷ 4/6

**5.** 2 1/3 ÷ ¾

**6.** ¾ ÷ 2 1/3

**7.** 2 ¾ ÷ 1.5

**8.** -6 ÷ 1/3

**9.** -1 /3 ÷ -6

**10.** -2 1/5 ÷ 10

**11.** 8 ÷ .4

**12.** -8 ÷ 2 ½

**13.** 6 ÷ -2

**14.** -2 ÷ -10

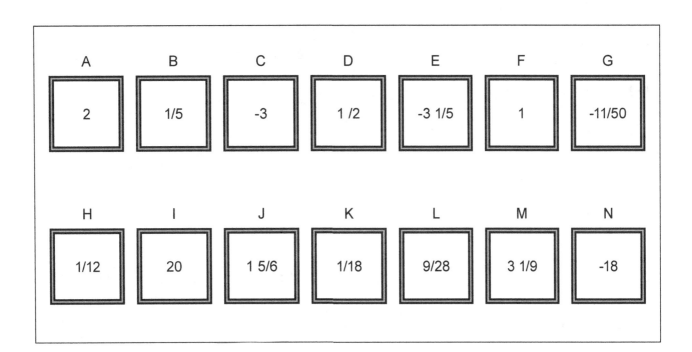

| A | B | C | D | E | F | G |
|---|---|---|---|---|---|---|
| 2 | 1/5 | -3 | 1 /2 | -3 1/5 | 1 | -11/50 |

| H | I | J | K | L | M | N |
|---|---|---|---|---|---|---|
| 1/12 | 20 | 1 5/6 | 1/18 | 9/28 | 3 1/9 | -18 |

**1.** _____    **2.** _____    **3.** _____    **4.** _____    **5.** _____    **6.** _____    **7.** _____

**8.** _____    **9.** _____    **10.** _____    **11.** _____    **12.** _____    **13.** _____    **14.** _____

# Dividing Integers and Rational Numbers 3

**Name** _____     **Date** _____

**Directions**: Solve the problems on the left side. Find the answers on the right side. Write the letter of the correct answer on the lines beside the numerals below.

| | | | | | |
|---|---|---|---|---|---|
| 1.) $10 \div 1\ 1/2$ | 2.) $7/8 \div -2/3$ | | **A** | **B** | **C** **D** |
| | | | $6\ 2/3$ | $4$ | $8$ $.1$ |
| 3.) $.2 \div \frac{1}{2}$ | 4.) $\frac{3}{4} \div -6$ | | **E** | **F** | **G** **H** |
| | | | $-1$ | $-5$ | $\frac{1}{2}$ $-1/8$ |
| 5.) $3/6$ | 6.) $-4 \div -1/2$ | | | | |
| | | | **I** | **J** | **K** **L** |
| 7.) $10/-2$ | 8.) $-6 \div 2\ 2/3$ | | $-1\ \frac{1}{2}$ | $-1\ 5/16$ | $-20$ $-2$ |
| 9.) $-3 \div 4 \div \frac{1}{2}$ | 10.) $2\ \frac{1}{2} \div 1\ 1/3$ | | | | |
| | | | **M** | **N** | **O** **P** |
| 11.) $-6 \div 3/4$ | 12.) $\frac{3}{4} \div -3/4$ | | $-8$ | $1\ 7/8$ | $-16$ $-8/9$ |
| 13.) $-4 / .2$ | 14.) $6 / -3$ | | **Q** | **R** | |
| 15.) $-4 \div 4\ 1/2$ | 16.) $-8 \div \frac{1}{2}$ | | $-2\ \frac{1}{4}$ | $.4$ | |
| 17.) $3 \div 6/8$ | 18.) $.04 \div .4$ | | | | |

1. _____  2. _____  3. _____  4. _____  5. _____  6. _____  7. _____

8. _____  9. _____  10. _____  11. _____  12. _____  13. _____  14. _____

15. _____  16. _____  17. _____  18. _____

# Dividing Integers and Rational Numbers 4

**Name** _____     **Date** _____

**Directions**: Cut out each rectangle. Start with 8 / 4. Find the answer on the next rectangle. Then connect the two rectangles with tape. Continue until all rectangles are connected.

| | | | |
|---|---|---|---|
| START | 8 / 4 | 7 | 2 1/3 ÷ 2 1/2 |
| 2 | 4 / 8 | 12 | 2/3 ÷ 12 |
| 75 | .004/.4 | 42 | .02 ÷ .84 |
| -1 | 6 ÷ 3 2/4 | 1/12 | -1/2 ÷ 2/4 |
| 14/15 | 2 2/5 ÷ 1/5 | 01 | END |
| -12 | 1/2 ÷ 6 | | |
| 1/ 42 | 250 ÷ 3 1/3 | | |
| 1/2 | -6 ÷ 1/2 | | |
| 1/ 18 | .84 ÷ .02 | | |
| 1 5/7 | 2 1/3 ÷ 1/3 | | |

# Dividing Integers and Rational Numbers 5

**Name** _____  **Date** _____

**Directions**: Find the stock market changes in the following days. Place the answers in the boxes on the left side.

| 4.1 | -8 1/5 ÷ - 2 | Monday |
|-----|--------------|--------|
|     | -4.5 ÷ .2 | Tuesday |
|     | 8 ÷ -.2 | Wednesday |
|     | -3 2/4 ÷ 2 2/3 ÷ -2 1/6 | Thursday |
|     | -2 ¾ ÷ -3 1/3 ÷ -1/2 | Friday |
|     | ( 60 ÷ -3 2/3 ) ÷ -4 | Saturday |
|     | -120 ÷ (-4 / -2 ) | Sunday |
|     | ( 2 1/5 ÷ 1/3) ÷ -6 | Monday |
|     | -2 1/3 ÷ -2 2/3 | Tuesday |
|     | -3 2/3 ÷ 2/4 | Wednesday |
|     | 3 ¼ ÷ 6 | Thursday |
|     | -9 ÷ -2 1/3 | Friday |

# Adding, Subtracting, Multiplying and Dividing Fractions

Name _____     Date _____

**Directions:** Find the answers to these examples.

**1.** $3/6 + 4/6$

**2.** $3/8 - 4/6$

**3.** $3/8 \times 20/18$

**4.** $3/8 \, / \, 6/12$

**5.** $3/a + 2/2a$

**6.** $2/4a - 7/a^2$

**7.** $(A^5B^3C^2/A^9B^4C^{10}) \cdot (A^2B^3C^7/A^6B^7C^7)$

**8.** $3a^6/8b^3 \div 10a^{10}/12a^7$

**9.** $(3B + 9) \div (6B^3 + 18B^2)$

**10.** $(a + b)/(a+b)^2 \div (a + b)^3/(a-b)^2$

**11.** $3/(a + 2) - 4/(a + 2)^2$

**12.** $2a \div 3a^4 + 2a \div 4b$

**13.** $(a+b)/(a+b)^2 \div (a+b)^3/(a+b)^2$

**14.** $(1 + 1/a) \div (2 - 2/a^2)$

**1.**

**2.**

**3.**

**4.**

**5.**

**6.**

**7.**

**8.**

**9.**

**10.**

**11.**

**12.**

**13.**

**14.**

# Chapter 3

# Operations, Equations, Inequalities and Absolute Values

# Order of Operations 1

**Name** _____     **Date** _____

**Directions**: Place addition or multiplication signs between 2, 8, 3, and 4. Use parentheses in all problems. Use your own paper to solve the problems.

(A).   2   8   3   4        (B).   2   8   3   4        (C).   2   8   3   4

(D).   2   8   3   4        (E).   2   8   3   4        (F).   2   8   3   4

(G).   2   8   3   4        (H).   2   8   3   4        ( I ).   2   8   3   4

(J).   2   8   3   4        (K).   2   8   3   4        (L).   2   8   3   4

(M).   2   8   3   4        (N).   2   8   3   4        (P).   2   8   3   4

# Order of Operations 2

Name _____     Date _____

**Directions**: Place addition or subtraction signs between 2, 8, 3, and 4. Use parentheses in all problems. Use your own paper to solve the problems.

(A).  2   8   3   4          (B).  2   8   3   4          (C).  2   8   3   4

(D).  2   8   3   4          (E).  2   8   3   4          (F).  2   8   3   4

(G).  2   8   3   4          (H).  2   8   3   4          (I).  2   8   3   4

(J).  2   8   3   4          (K).  2   8   3   4          (L).  2   8   3   4

(M).  2   8   3   4          (N).  2   8   3   4          (P).  2   8   3   4

# Order of Operations 3

**Directions:** Solve these problems by using addition , subtraction ,and multiplication signs between 2, 8, 3, and -3. Use parentheses in all problems.

(A).  2  8  3  -3      (B).  2  8  3  -3      (C).  2  8  3  -3

(D).  2  8  3  -3      (E).  2  8  3  -3      (F).  2  8  3  -3

(G).  2  8  3  -3      (H).  2  8  3  -3      (I).  2  8  3  -3

(J).  2  8  3  -3      (K).  2  8  3  -3      (L).  2  8  3  -3

# Order of Operations 4

**Name** _____     **Date** _____

**Directions:** Use the next page to complete this assignment. Work in groups of twos to solve the order of operations problems. Place the steps by the problems.

**1.** *Write the  problem.*

**2.** *Do the operations inside the parentheses, brackets ,and  fraction bars.*

**3.** *Do all your powers.*

**4.** *Do all multiplications and divisions from  left to right.*

**5.** *Do additions and subtractions from left to right.*

**6.** *Write the answer.*

Example

$120 - (3)^2 \times 4 \div 6$            Given
$120 - (3)^2 x 4 \div 6$       Powers
$120 - 9 \times 4 \div 6$       Multiply from Left to right.
$120 - 36 \div 6$       Divide from left to right.
$120 - 6$       Subtract.
$114$       Write the answers.

# Order of Operations 5

**Name** _____   **Date** _____

**Directions**: Use example 4 from the previous page. Place the steps beside each part of the problems.

**(A).** $2 ( 3 - 2 )^2 + 20 \div 4$ _____
$2 ( 3 - 2 )^2 + 20 \div 4$ _____
$2 ( 1 )^2 + 20 \div 4$ _____
$2 + 20 \div 4$ _____
$2 + 5$ _____
$7$ _____
_____

**(B).** $2 ( 3 + 2 )^2 \times 20 \div 4$ _____
$2 ( 3 + 2 )^2 \times 20 \div 4$ _____
$2 ( 5^2 ) \times 20 \div 4$ _____
$2 \times 25 \times 20 \div 4$ _____
$50 \times 20 \div 4$ _____
$1000 \div 4$ _____
$250$ _____

**(C).** $2 ( 4 + -3 + 2 ) 2 \div 4$ _____
$2 ( 4 + -3 + 2 ) 2 \div 4$ _____
$2 ( 3 ) 2 \div 4$ _____
$6 \times 2 \div 4$ _____
$12 \div 4$ _____
$3$ _____

**(D).** $3 + 2 \times 3 + 5$ _____
$3 + 2 \times 3 + 5$ _____
$3 + 6 + 5$ _____
$9 + 5$ _____
$14$ _____

**(E).** $29 - 3 ( 9 - 4 )$ _____
$29 - 3 ( 9 - 4 )$ _____
$29 - 3 ( 5 )$ _____
$29 - 15$ _____
$14$ _____

**(F).** $15 \div 3 \times 5 - 4^2$ _____
$15 / 3 \times 5 - 4^2$ _____
$15 / 3 \times 5 - 16$ _____
$5 \times 5 - 16$ _____
$25 - 16$ _____
$9$ _____

**(G).** $( 5 - 1 )^2 + ( 11 - 2 )^2 + ( 7 - 4 )^2$ _____
$( 5 - 1 )^2 + ( 11 - 2 )^2 + ( 7 - 4 )^2$ _____
$4^2 + 9^2 + 3^2$ _____
$16 + 81 + 9$ _____
$97 + 9$ _____
$106$ _____

# Order of Operations 6

**Directions**: Use your own paper to make needed corrections. Some of the problems are correctly solved. Do not rewrite the correct problems.

### A

$- 3 + 12 \div 4 - 8 \times 2 + 5 \times 3$
$-3 + 3 - 16 + 15$
$0 - 16 + 15$
$- 16 + 15$
$-1$

### B

$3 ( 3 + 5 ) - 2 ( 1 - 5 ) \div ( 2 + 6 )$
$3 ( 8 ) - 2 \times - 4 \div 8$
$24 + 8 \div 8$
$32 \div 8$
$4$

### C

$8 + 2 \times 8 - 10 + 4 \times 2$
$8 + 12 - 10 + 8$
$20 + -10 + 8$
$2 + 8$
$10$

### D

$12/3 + -2 + 7 - 4 \times 5^2$
$12/3 + -2 + 7 - 4 \times 25$
$4 + -2 + 7 + -100$
$2 + 7 + -100$
$9 + -100$
$-81$

### E

$( 2 \times 5 + 4 + -8 ) \div 2$
$( 2 \times 9 + -8 ) \div 2$
$10 \div 2$
$5$

### F

$2 ( 7 - 5 )^3 \, 2 \div 4 + 2$
$2 \times 2^3 \times 2 \div 4 + 2$
$( 2 \times 8 \times 2 ) \div 4 + 2$
$32 \div 4 + 2$
$8 + 2$
$16$

### G

$1/2 ( 4 - 2 ) \, 3 \div 3$
$1/2 \times 2 \times 2 \times 3 \div 3$
$1/2 \times 2 \times 3 \div 3$
$1 \times 3 \div 3$
$3/3$
$1$

### H

$2 ( 8 - 2 )^3 \, 4 \div 2$
$2 \times 6^3 \times 4 \div 2$
$2 \times 216 \times 4 \div 2$
$218 \times 4 \div 2$
$872 \div 2$
$436$

# Order of Operations 7

**Directions**: Use the letters beside each group of boxes to arrange each step in the problem in proper sequence. Write the proper sequence on the lines below the boxes.

**(1)**

A | 2 + 3 + 5 |

B | 10 |

C | 5 + 5 |

__ __ __

**(2)**

A | 3 + 2 + 5 + 7 |

B | 17 |

C | 5 + 5 + 7 |

D | 10 + 7 |

__ __ __ __ __

**(3)**

A | 3 - 2 + 6 - 8 |

B | -1 |

C | 7 - 8 |

D | 1 + 6 - 8 |

__ __ __ __ __ __

**(4)**

A | 10 X 2 ÷ 2 X 6 / 2 |

B | 60 / 2 |

C | 20 / 2 x 6 / 2 |

D | 30 |

E | 10 x 6 / 2 |

__ __ __ __ __

**(5)**

A | 2 + 3 x 2 - 4 |       D | 2 + 6 - 4 |

B | 4 |

C | 8 - 4 |       __ __ __ __

# Order of Operations 8

**Name** _____  **Date** _____

**Directions**: Find the temperature in each state by solving the order of operations. Write answers below the expressions.

**1.** Washington State

$20 + 3 ( 5 \times 2 )^2 \div 2^3$

_____

**2.** North Dakota

$3 ( 8 - 2 )^2 \div 4$

_____

**3.** Pennsylvania

$200 ( 2 ) \div 4$

_____

**4.** New York

$3 ( 6 - 2 )^2 \, 5 \div 2 \times 4$

_____

**5.** California

$100 \div 10 \times 2^3$

_____

**6.** Utah

$80 \div 2^2 \div 2 \div 4 \times 2^3$

_____

**7.** Kentucky

$120 - 5 ( 5 - 2 )^2$

_____

**8.** South Carolina

$100 \div 2^2 + 20 \div 4$

_____

**9.** Texas

$( 200 \div 4 )^2 / 5^2$

_____

**10.** Florida

$3 ( 2 \times 3 )^2$

_____

# Order of Operations 9

**Name** _____   **Date** _____

**Directions**: Solve each algebraic expression. Which beverage belongs in each container. Write the letter of the correct container on each line.

**1.** $3 \times 2 - 5 \times 3 / 9$     Lemonade _____

**2.** $( 2 ) 6 \div ( 3 \times 4 )$     Coffee _____

**3.** $( 7 - 4 )^3 \times 4$     Latte _____

**4.** $( 5 - 8 )^4 / 4$     Soda _____

**5.** $2 ( 3 - 2 ) 2 \div 4$     Water _____

**6.** $[ 2 ( 6 + 2 ) 2 ] \div [ 3 ( 6 - 5 ) / 2 ]$     Milk _____

**7.** $( 9 - 6 ) \div ( 10 - 4 )$     Tea _____

**8.** $\{ [ 2000 \div 10^0 ] \div 10^3 \} \times ( 3^4 - 50 )$     Punch _____

**9.** $( 8^3 + 4^2 ) \times 3^2 \div 2^2 \times 28 + 10^2$     Coffee _____

**10.** $( 2 \times 3 \times 4 \times 2 ) / 4^3$     Juice _____

A = 62

B = 20 1/4

C = 33364

D = 20

E = 21 1/3

F = 2

G = 4 1/3     H = 108     I = 1 /2     V = 1     J = 3/4

# Order of Operations 10

Name _____     Date _____

**Directions:** Find the number of people in each room.

| | | |
|---|---|---|
| Porch<br>$(6 + 3 - 7) \div 2$ | Bedroom 3<br>$(7 + 19 - 6 \times 2) \div 2$ | Bedroom 2<br>$(3 + 3 \times 2 \times 3 + 4 - 2 \times -5)$ |
| Library<br>$(200 \div 10 / 5 + 2$ | Family Room<br>$(6/4)(2/6)(20)(3/2)$ | Powder Room<br>$(100/2)/ 10$ |
| Linen Closet<br>$(10\ 2/3 \times 3/.4)$ | | Theater<br>$(400/40) \div 5 + 9$ |
| Sunroom<br>$(160 \div 4^2)$ | Kitchen<br>$(100/2) + 3$ | Dining Room<br>$2 (10 + 5 - 6) /3$ |
| | Pantry<br>$2 + 6(9 -3)^3 - 2$ | Bathroom 2<br>$(2 + 3)(10 - 6)^3 - 10^2$ |

Porch _____     Family Room _____

Library _____     Kitchen _____

Linen Closet _____     Bedroom 2 _____

Sunroom _____     Theater _____

Bedroom 3 _____     Dining Room _____

# Equations 1

**Name** _____     **Date** _____

**Directions**: Solve each equation. Use a ruler to draw a line to represent each given length in inches. Use a separate sheet of paper to draw the lines. Be sure to label each line.

1. $2X = 10$

2. $2X = 1$

3. $.2X = 1$

4. $2X = 1 / 2$

5. $2X = 10 \ 1 / 2$

6. $.2X = .6$

7. $3X = 3/8$

8. $1/2X = 1$

9. $1/2X = 2.5$

10. $1/2X = 1 \ /2$

11. $1/2X = 1 \ 1 / 2$

12. $2 \ \frac{1}{2} X = 10$

13. $X + 3 = 3$

14. $X - 3 = 3$

15. $X + 3 = 6$

16. $X + 3 = 4$

17. $X - 3 = -3$

18. $X - .3 = 4.7$

19. $X + .6 = 6.6$

20. $X + 3.5 = 7$

21. $X + 3.5 = 8.5$

22. $X + 1 / 2 = 4$

23. $X + 1 / 2 = 3$

24. $X + 4 \ 1 / 2 = 8 \ 3 / 4$

25. $X - 3 \ 1/8 = 3 \ 3 / 4$

26. $X - 8.3 = -3.8$

# Equations 2

Name _____ Date _____

**Directions**: Solve each equation and find as many answers as you can in the basket. Can you make the basket? If you can make the basket, color the correct answer in the basket. Write Y for yes and N for no on the lines below.

**A.**

$X + 8 = -1$

**B.**

$2X + 2 = -10$

**C.**

$2X - 3 = -8$

**D.**

$2x + 4 = -8$

**E.**

$-X - 4 = -6$

**F.**

$.2X = -2$

**G.**

$X/2 = 4$

**H.**

$-X + 3 = 7$

**I.**

$X/2 = -4$

**J.**

$X + .5 = .75$

**K.**

$-X = -1/3$

**L.**

$-X = -4$

**M.**

$X/2 = 3/2$

**N.**

$X/-3 = 4$

**O.**

$X + 4.7 = 653$

**P.**

$6X - 6.8 = 87.5$

**Q**

$-8X + 54.6 = -76.4$

Basket values:
15.7
-15, -6, -1, -12
-8, 7, -9
6, 1 ¼, 9, 12
-4, 6, 16
7 ¼, 3, 5, 7
-1, -4, 3/5
1.6, -3, 2.5, 11
20, 15, 3
10, 2, -3, -7
-7, .25, 8, 11
-11, 4, 2

A. _____   B. _____   C. _____   D. _____   E. _____   F. _____   G. _____

H. _____   I. _____   J. _____   K. _____   L. _____   M. _____   N. _____

O. _____   P. _____   Q. _____

# Equations or Formulas 3

**Name** _____    **Date** _____

**Directions**: Solve these equations for 1. (A)   2. (F)   3. (r)   4. (H)   5. (r)   6. (b₁)   7. (W)   8. (r)   9. (r)   10. (X)   11. (r)

1. $C = 2A + 2B$

2. $C = 5/9(F - 32)$

3. $C = 2(3.14)(r)$

4. $C = 1/2 \, BH$

5. $C = 3.14 \, r^2 H$

6. $C = 1/2h(b_1 + b_2)$

7. $C = LWH$

8. $C = rt$

9. $C = 1/3(3.14)r^2$

10. $C = 2/3X + 8$

11. $C = 2(3.14)rh + 2B$

# Equations 4

**Name** _____     **Date** _____

**Directions**: Solve the equations for "X". Shade your answers.

**1.** X + 5 = 7      **2.** X + 5 = 3      **3.** X + 4.5 = 9      **4.** X + 3.3 = 2.3

**5.** X + 2/3 = -2/4      **6.** X - 1/6 = 8      **7.** X - 6 = -7      **8.** X -8 = - 5.6

**9.** X - 2 2/5 = 4 2/9      **10.** X - 4 2/5 = 1 /3      **11.** X - 3/6 = 3/8      **12.** X + 6 ¾ = ½

**13.** X + 3/6 = 14      **14.** X + 5 = 3.6      **15.** X - 2/8 = 5/12      **16.** X + 5 = 10 3/6

**17.** X + 54 = 54.4      **18.** X - 128 = -234      **19.** X + 4.8 = 7.90      **20.** X +43 2/8 = 25 2/4

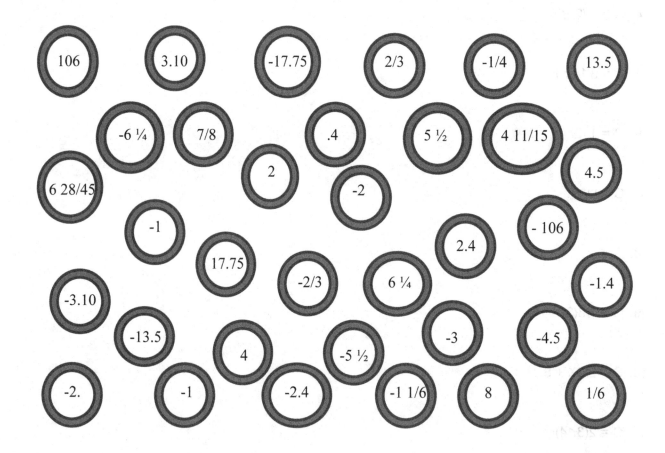

70

# Equations 5

**Directions**: Solve these equations with variables on both sides. Find the number of answers for the following numbers.

| 6 | -6 | -18 | 18 | 2 4/7 | -2 4/7 | -6/7 | 6/7 |
|---|----|-----|----|-------|--------|------|-----|
| _____ | _____ | _____ | _____ | _____ | _____ | _____ | _____ |

**1.** $3X + 6 = 4X + 12$     **2.** $-3X - 6 = -4X - 12$     **3.** $3X - 6 = 4X + 12$     **4.** $3X - 6 = -4X + 12$

**5.** $3X - 6 = 4X - 12$     **6.** $-3X + 6 = 4X - 12$     **7.** $3X + 6 = 4X - 12$     **8.** $4X - 6 = 3X - 12$

**9.** $3X + 6 = -4X - 12$     **10.** $3X - 6 = -4X - 12$     **11.** $-3X + 6 = 4X + 12$     **12.** $-3X - 6 = 4X - 12$

**13.** $4X - 6 = 3X - 12$     **14.** $-4X + 6 = -3X + 12$     **15.** $-3X + 6 = -4x - 12$     **16.** $-3X - 6 = -4X - 12$

**17.** $-4X - 6 = 3X + 12$     **18.** $3X - 6 = 4X + 12$     **19.** $4X - 6 = -3X + 12$     **20.** $4X - 12 = 3x - 6$

# Equations 6

Name _____        Date _____

**Directions**: Solve the equations by using the distributive property. Circle the correct answers below.

**1.** $3(X - 3) = 8$        **2.** $-2(X + 4) = -10$        **3.** $\frac{1}{2}(X + 4) = 8$        **4.** $-2/3(X - 6) = 18$

**5.** $X/3 - 2/3 = 4/3$        **6.** $X/3 + 2X/4 = 8$        **7.** $2X/3 + 1/8X = \frac{1}{2}$        **8.** $3(X + 2.1) = 9.3$

**9.** $3(X + 4) = 6(X - 4)$        **10.** $-3(X - 4) = 2(X - 2)$        **11.** $2/3(X + 4) = 7.2$        **12.** $-3/5(X - 3) = 1/3$

**13.** $\frac{1}{2}(X + 3) = 6$        **14.** $3X + \frac{1}{2}(X + 7) = 8$        **15.** $2\frac{1}{2}(X + 3) = 4$        **16.** $X + 4(X - 4) = -64$

5 2/4     -22     23.4     13     9/16     11     3 1/4     - 1 2/6

1     15     14     8.6     -2 4/9     6.9     -2

6.8     -2 4/8     9.6     3 1/5     8     9     7

12     9     6     9     -21     12

8.9     5 2/3     23.43     0

-6     -76     -53     -4.5

-9     -3 1/5     10

-10     -7     -5

6.9

# Equations 7

Name _____    Date _____

**Directions**: Solve these equations by substituting the answers in the boxes.

**1.**

$2X = 6$

**2.**

$-3X = 12$

**3.**

$2X = -24$

**4.**

$1 / 2 X = 1$

**5.**

$2X = 1/3$

**6.**

$7 /8 X = 1 / 4$

**7.**

$2.2 X = 40.4$

**8.**

$-3 /5 X = 4$

# Equations 8

**Name** _____     **Date** _____

**Directions**: Write the letters above the answers in the boxes below. Some answers are not needed. Solve the equations to decode the four types of cars.


**1.** F $2X + 5 = 3X - 8$

**2.** N $.3( X - 60 ) = 9.3$

**3.** O $1 / 2 ( X - 5 ) = -23$

**4.** G $2X + 3X - 7 = -4X + 2X + 9$

**5.** E $X / 3 + 1/ 2 = X / 6 - X / 4$

**6.** A $2X = 4 \ 1/ 4$

**7.** D $2 / 3 (x + 6) = 1 / 4$

**8.** R $2(X + 3 ) = 8$

**9.** L $3 / 4 X = 3 / 5$

**10.** V $.2 ( X + 4) = .2 ( X - 4.2)$

**11.** S $x / 4 = 12 / 8$

**12.** T $3X + 6 = 3 (X + 1) + 3$


| 13 | -41 | 1 | - 5 5/8 |
|----|-----|---|---------|

| - 5 5/8 | - 41 | - 5 5/8 | 2 2/7 | - 1 1/5 |
|---------|------|---------|-------|---------|

| 2 1/8 | No Solution | 2 1/8 | 4/5 | -41 | 91 |
|-------|-------------|-------|-----|-----|----|

| 6 | -41 | 91 | 2 1/8 | All real Numbers | 2 1/8 |
|---|-----|----|-------|------------------|-------|

# Equations 9

Name _____     Date _____

**Directions**: Solve these equations by substituting the answers in the squares. The correct number of squares is given.

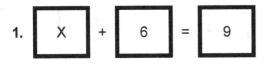

1. [ X ] + [ 6 ] = [ 9 ]

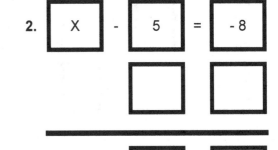

2. [ X ] - [ 5 ] = [ - 8 ]

3. [ X ] + [ 20 ] = [ -26 ]

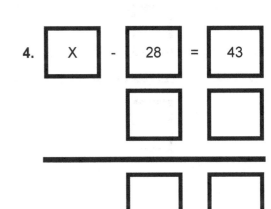

4. [ X ] - [ 28 ] = [ 43 ]

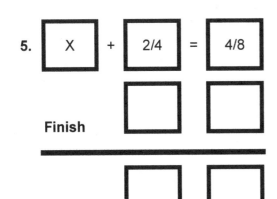

5. [ X ] + [ 2/4 ] = [ 4/8 ]

Finish

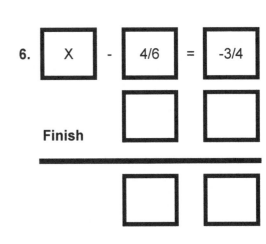

6. [ X ] - [ 4/6 ] = [ -3/4 ]

Finish

# Equations 10

**Name** _____     **Date** _____

**Directions**: Solve these equations by substituting the answers in the squares. The correct number of squares are given.

**A.**  $\boxed{9X}$ - $\boxed{3}$ = $\boxed{8X}$ - $\boxed{2}$        **B.**  $\boxed{-8X}$ + $\boxed{6}$ = $\boxed{10X}$ + $\boxed{7}$

$\square$        $\square$                                 $\square$        $\square$

$\square$  $\square$        $\square$              $\square$  $\square$        $\square$

$\square$        $\square$              $\square$  $\square$        $\square$

$\square$        $\square$              $\square$              $\square$

$\square$              $\square$

$\square$              $\square$

# Equations 11

**Directions**: Substitute the numbers and variables in the boxes. Solve these equations.

**1.**  | 3 ( X + 2 ) |  =  | 2 ( X - 2) |

☐ + ☐ = ☐ + ☐

☐ = ☐

─────────────

☐ = ☐ ☐

☐ ☐

─────────────

☐ = ☐

**2.**  | 3/5 ( X + 3 ) |  =  | 3 |

☐ + ☐ = ☐

( ☐ + ☐ = ☐ )

☐ + ☐ = ☐

☐ = ☐

─────────────

☐ = ☐

☐ = ☐

77

# Equations 12

Name _____     Date _____

**Directions**: Solve the equations. Color the answers using the designated colors.

1.    X - 3 = 21          2.    2X - 2 = 78          3.    -2X + 4 = 386          4.    1/2X -2 = 3
         Tan                          Yellow                       Blue                            Red

5.    ( X + 2) / 2 = 4     6.    X = 0          7.    2/3( X + 2 ) + 6 = 180     8.    2X - 40 = 80
         Green                      Purple                    Orange                          Black

9.    2(X - 6) = 8(X + 8)   10.    X/2 + -3/4 = 3   11.    ( X + 2 )/2 = (X - 2)/ 3   12.    .2X = 50
         Red                          Red                        Green                           Blue

| 24 | 7.5 | 40 |
|----|-----|----|

| 250 | -191 | -10 |
|-----|------|-----|

| 259 | -12 2/3 | 6 |
|-----|---------|---|

| 10 | 0 | 60 |
|----|---|----|

# Inequalities 1

**Name** _____    **Date** _____

**Directions**: Use symbols to solve inequalities.

| Problems | Add | Subtract | Multiply | Divide | Distributive Law | Answer |
|----------|-----|----------|----------|--------|------------------|--------|
|  | | | | | | |
| A | B | C | D | E | F | G |

**1.** $X + 5 > 10$

**2.** $X - 5 \leq 8$

**3.** $2X < -41$

**4.** $2/3X > 6$

**5.** $-3/7X < -9$

**6.** $3\ 2/8\ X > \frac{1}{2}$

**7.** $-4X \leq 3\ 2/6$

**8.** $2X + 3 > X + 9$

**9.** $2/3X < 6 + X$

**10.** $2/3( X - 3 ) > 1/3$

**11.** $5( X + 4 ) < 3( X + 6 )$

**12.** $2X + 4X - 5 + 7 \geq -4X + 3X - 10$

**13.** $1/3X + 4 \leq 1/6X - 7$

# Inequalities 2

**Name** _____ **Date** _____

**Directions**: Cut out each domino. Solve the inequality inside the rectangles on the right.

Connect the problems with tape or draw the rectangles with the answer on the pages.

| | | | |
|---|---|---|---|
| $X \geq -5$ | $X + 2 \geq 6$ | $X \geq 0$ | $7X - 1 \leq 6X + 6$ |
| Blank/Start | $X + 3 \geq 4$ | $X \leq 6$ | $X - 1.1 \geq -2$ |
| $X \leq 3/8$ | $10 \geq X + 8$ | $X \geq 2$ | $-9 + X \geq 9$ |
| $X \geq 18$ | $X - 7 \geq -12$ | $X \geq -3/4$ | $X + 1/8 \leq 1/2$ |
| $X \leq 2$ | $2X \leq X + 1$ | $X \geq -.9$ | $X + \frac{1}{2} \geq -1/4$ |
| $X \geq 4$ | $2X + 4 \geq 4$ | $X \leq -18$ | Finish |
| $X \geq 0$ | $X + 7 \geq 2$ | $X \geq 1$ | $X - 2 \leq 4$ |
| $X \leq 1$ | $2X + 3 \geq X + 5$ | $X \leq 7$ | $-X + 11 \geq 29$ |

80

# Inequalities 3

**Directions**: Write the correct sequence of the steps on the lines below the problems.

**1a.**  $3X + 3 > X + 4$

e. $X > 1/2$

g. $-X > -X$

b. $2x/2 > \frac{1}{2}$

d. $3X > 1 + X$

c. $-3 > -3$

f. $2X > 1$

**1a.** __ __ __ __ __ __

**2a.**  $\frac{1}{2}(X - 4) \leq 3(X + 3)$

k. $x \geq -4\ 2/5$

g. $x \leq 6x + 22$

b. $-5x \leq 22$

t. $-5x/-5 \leq 22/-5$

e. $-6x \leq -6x$

c. $2(1/2x + 2(-2) \leq 2(3x) + 2(9)$

d. $4 \leq 4$

r. $1/2x - 2 \leq 3x + 9$

s. $x - 4 \leq 6x + 18$

**2a.** __ __ __ __ __ __ __ __ __ __

**3a.**  $-5X + 2 \leq 18$

h. $-2 < -2$

f. $-5X \leq 16$

l. $X \geq -3\ 1/5$

J. $-5X / -5 \leq 16/-5$

**4a.**  $\frac{1}{2}(X + 4) + 3X - 5X \leq 1/3X - 3$

b. $X \geq 2\ 8/11$

h. $-2 \leq -2$

d. $-9X \leq 2X - 30$

k. $1/2X - 2X \leq 1/3X - 5$

g. $-2X \leq -2X$

c. $1/2X + 2 + 3X - 5X \leq 1/3X - 3$

w. $-11X \leq -30$

f. $3X - 12X \leq 2X - 30$

e. $-11/-11 \leq -30/-11$

t. $1/2X + 2 - 2X \leq 1/3X - 3$

y. $6(1/2x) + 6(-2x) \leq 6(1/3x) + 6(-5)$

**3a.** __ __ __ __ __ __ __ __

**4a.** __ __ __ __ __ __ __ __ __ __ __

# Inequalities 4

Name _____     Date _____

**Directions**: Write the correct sequence of the steps on the lines below the problems.

**1 a.** X + 3 > 4

**b.** X + 0 > 1

**c.** X > 1

**d.** -3 > -3

\_\_ \_\_ \_\_ \_\_

**2 a.** X - 3 ≤ -4

**b.** X ≤ -1

**c.** X + 0 ≤ -1

**d.** 3 ≤ 3

\_\_ \_\_ \_\_ \_\_

**3 a.** X - 3 > -1

**b.** 3 > 3

**c.** X + 0 > 2

**d.** X > 2

\_\_ \_\_ \_\_ \_\_

**4 a.** -2X ≥ 10

**b.** X < -5

**c.** -2X/ -2 ≥10 /-2

\_\_ \_\_ \_\_ \_\_

**5 a.** − X ≥ 6

**b.** X ≤ -6

\_\_ \_\_ \_\_ \_\_

**6 a.** 2X < 10

**b.** X < 5

**c.** 2X /2 < 10 /2

\_\_ \_\_ \_\_ \_\_

**7 a.** 1/3X + 4 ≥ 1/2X + 6

**b.** X ≤ -12

**c.** 6( 1/3X + 4) ≥ 6( 1/2X + 6 )

**d.** -3X ≥ - 3X

**e.** -24 ≥ -24

**f.** 2X + 24 ≥ 3X + 36

**g.** -1X ≥ 12

**h.** -1X + 24 ≥ 36

\_\_ \_\_ \_\_ \_\_

**8 a.** -1/3X < - 7

**b.** X > 21

**c.** -1X /-1 < -21 / -1

**d.** 3(-1/3X) < 3(-7)

\_\_ \_\_ \_\_ \_\_

# Solving Inequalities 5

Name _____     Date _____

**Directions**: Solve these inequalities. The person who finds the most answers wins the game. Color the answers on the left side red and color the answers on the right side green.

### LEFT SIDE

**1.** $3X + 1 - 4X < -3$

**2.** $1/2X > -8$

**3.** $2/3 + X > 5/6$

**4.** $-5(X - 4) > X + 2$

**5.** $-X > 8$

**6.** $.2(X - 4) > 8$

**7.** $6X + 7 < 6X - 3$

**8.** $-2/3 > 8X$

### RIGHT SIDE

**9.** $-3(X - 1) > 2X + 6$

**10.** $¾ + 2/3X < X - ¾$

**11.** $2X - 6 < X - 8$

**12.** $6X + 7 < 6X + 3$

**13.** $6X + 7 > 6X + 2$

**14.** $-3X - 7 > X + 13$

**15.** $4X - 5X + 2X ≥ 5X + 4X + 15$

**16.** $X + 1/3 ≤ 1/10 - 2X$

### Left Side

| X > 4 | X > -5 | X < -7/9 | X < -3/5 |
|-------|--------|----------|----------|
| X < -2 | All real numbers | X > -16 | X > -8 |
| X > 3 | X > 1/6 | X < 0 | X < 5 |
| X < 3 | X < -1/6 | X > 0 | X > 7.5 |
| X < 1 | Ø | X < -4 | X > 44 |

### Right Side

| X < 4 | Ø | X > 1/6 | All real numbers |
|-------|---|---------|------------------|
| X > -2 | X < -7/9 | X > 2 | X > -7/9 |
| X > 0 | X > -3/5 | X < 8 | X < -7.5 |
| X < -3 | Ø | X > -4 | X > 2 |
| X > 9 | X > 4.5 | X > 1 | X < -2 |

83

# Inequalities 6

**Name** _____   **Date** _____

**Directions**: Graph the "OR" statements in inequalities and connect the open circles.

1. X < 0 or X > 0        2. X < -4 or X > 4        3. X < -3 or X > 3

4. X < -6 or X > 6        5. X < -4 or X > 4        6. X < -3 or X > 3

7. X < -3 or X > 3        8. X < -2 or X > 2        9. X < -3 or X > 3

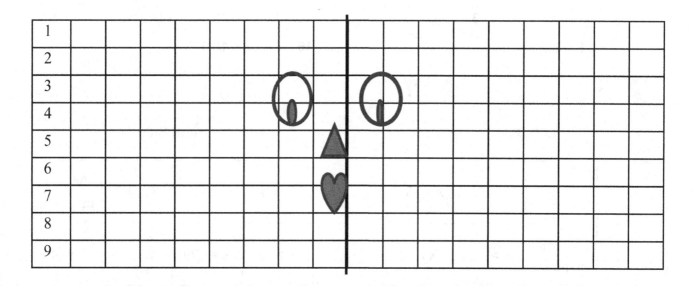

# Inequalities 7

Name _____ Date _____

**Directions**: Graph the "And" statements in inequalities. Connect the closed circles. Use the graph at the bottom. On the left side of the graph, write your numbers from 1 to 8.

**1.** $-3 \leq X \leq 3$    **2.** $-4 \leq X \leq 4$    **3.** $-5.5 \leq X \leq 5.5$    **4.** $-5 \leq X \leq 5$

**5.** $-2 \leq X \leq 2$    **6.** $-2 \leq X \leq 2$    **7.** $-2 \leq X \leq 2$    **8.** $-2 \leq X \leq 2$

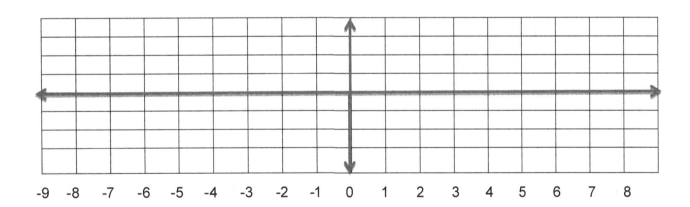

# Inequalities 8

**Directions**: Solve these inequalities. Show your work on your paper.

**1.** $2X \leq 6.006$

**2.** $-2X \geq -90$

**3.** $-5X > 3\ 2/4$

**4.** $-\frac{3}{4} X \leq 6$

**5.** $4/6\ X \geq 4/8$

**6.** $X/4 \leq 4/8$

**7.** $3X + 5 \geq 65$

**8.** $-5X - 4.8 < 8.96$

**9.** $3/6(\ X + 4\ ) \geq 90$

**10.** $-4/5(X + 4\ ) > 14$

**11.** $3(\ X + 7) > -7(\ X + 6)$

**12.** $3X - 8 \geq 8X - 45$

**13.** $-6X + 5 \leq 5X - 87$

**14.** $\frac{3}{4}(X - 6\ ) \geq X + 53$

**15.** $X/4 + 2/6 < X/5 - 2/2$

**16.** $2/4(\ X - 5\ ) \geq -5/3\ (\ X + 2\ )$

**17.** $X - 4X + 6 \geq -3X + 1$

**18.** $X/4 - X/5 \leq 3/5 - 1/2$

**19.** $5 + 3X - 3X - 6X > -5X + 3X - 12.2$

**20.** $2\frac{3}{4} X + 2/4 \leq 1\ 1/2\ X + -6$

# Inequalities 9

**Directions**: Solve the inequalities. Write answers on the lines. Color answers in the boxes for problems 1 to 6 red. Color answers in the boxes for problems 7 to 12 green.

**1.** Jack is at least 50 years old. _____

**2.** Jack is at most 50 years old. _____

**3.** Jack is no more than 7. _____

**4.** Jack is no more than 3. _____

**5.** Jack is less than or equal to three. _____

**6.** Six increased by x is greater than -2. _____

**7.** The difference of x and six is at least twenty. _____

**8.** Three times a number is more than twice the sum of a number and nine. _____

**9.** Three times a number is less than twice the sum of a number and nine. _____

**10.** The sum of three times a number and nine is less than twice the number. _____

**11.** Three times a number is at most thirty-six. _____

**12.** A number decreased by negative four is at most two. _____

| $J \leq 50$ | $J < 3$ | $6 + X > -2$ | $3X \geq 36$ | $X > 30$ |
|---|---|---|---|---|
| $J \geq 50$ | $J \geq 3$ | $X - 6 \leq 20$ | $3X \leq 36$ | $X \geq -30$ |
| $J < 7$ | $J \geq 80$ | $3N > 2(N+9)$ | $36 \geq 3N$ | $X > -43$ |
| $J \geq 7$ | $J \leq 80$ | $3N > 2(N-9)$ | $3X +9 < 2X$ | $X \leq 43$ |
| $J \geq 7$ | $J \leq 3$ | $N -(-4) \leq 2$ | $X - 6 > 20$ | $X < 49$ |

# Graphing Absolute Values

Name _____    Date _____

**Directions**: Solve the absolute values by writing the answers.

1. $|X + 2| = 5$ _____

2. $|2X + 2| = 2$ _____

3. $|X - 2| = 4$ _____

4. $|2X - 3| \geq 5$ _____

5. $|3X - 4| \leq 3$ _____

6. $|X + 2| \leq 4$ _____

7. $|6X - 2| \geq -6$ _____

8. $|X - 3| \leq -5$ _____

9. $|5 + 3X - 2| \leq 0$ _____

10. $|X| \leq 3$ _____

# Chapter 4

Exponents, Scientific Notation, Prime Factorization, and Greatest Common Factor

# Law of Exponents 1

Name _____     Date _____

**Directions**: Substitute the variables in the expressions below using a = 2 , b = 2 , and c = 3 . Solve the problems. Place the answers on the bar graph.

**1.)** $100abc^4$

**2.)** $36,000 \div (ab)$

**3.)** $(ac)^6c$

**4.)** $(abc)^4$

**5.)** $(ac)^6 \div 20$

**6.)** $30a^7$

**7.)** $(4ab)^4$

**8.)** $(4ab)^4 \div (ab)$

**9.)** $c^{18} \div c^{12}(100)$

**10.)** $(abc)^5$

**11.)** $(c^{10}) \div (b^4)$

**12.)** $a^5b^3c^6$

**13.)** $3(ab)^2(a^3b)^3$

**14.)** $\{(3(ab)^2(a^3b)^3\} \div b^4$

**15.)** $A^3b^0(23457)$

0  10 20 30 40 50 60 70 80 90 100 110 120 130 140 160 170 180 190 200 210 220 230 240 250 260

Thousands of People

# Laws of Exponents 2

Name _____     Date _____

**Directions**: Color in the correct answers. Write the letter of the problem in the box with its answer. All answers will not be found in the boxes.

**A.** $(2\ a^2b^2c^3)^3$

**B.** $(2\ a^3b^3c^4)^5$

**C.** $(2\ a^3b^2)^3\ (2\ a)^2$

**D.** $(2\ a\ b^6c\ )^2\ (-2a^2)^3$

**E.** $3(a^2b^3c)^2(2ab^3c^2)^3$

**F.** $(½\ a^2b^3c\ )^3(8a^3b^2c^2)$

**G.** $(-2\ a^3b^2c\ )(-3a^2b^3)^3$

**H.** $(1/2\ ab^3c^4)(1/4a^2b\ c\ )^2$

**I.** $2\ a^3b^2\ 1/2a^4b^3c^4$

**J.** $(2a^3b^4c^8)(3a^2b^3)$

**K.** $a\ a^2b\ a^3b^3$

**L.** $(a^2b^2)^2—(a^2b^2)^2$

**M.** $(1/3\ a^2b^3)(3/2\ a^3b^2)$

**N.** $(-2a^2b^3c^8)^5$

**O.** $(½\ a\ b\ c^4\ )^2$

**P.** $(3abc)(2abc)$

| | | | | | |
|---|---|---|---|---|---|
| $-108a^{12}b^{13}$ | $-6a^2b^3c^4$ | $1/256a^8b^{14}c^{18}$ | $6a^5b^7c^8$ | $-32\ a^8b^{12}c^2$ | $a^{20}b^6c$ |
| $32a^{15}b^{15}c^{20}$ | $-a^6b^4$ | $-32a^8b^{12}c^2$ | $-4a^3b\ c^{20}$ | $8a^6b^6c^9$ | $a^3b^2c^5$ |
| $20\ a^4b^6$ | $1/2a^5$ | $a^6b^4$ | $-\ 6\ a^3b^6c^8$ | $32a^{11}b^6$ | $0$ |
| $6a^2b^2c^2$ | $32a^9b^{11}c^5$ | $a^7b^5c^4$ | $1/4a^6b^7c^2$ | $-2ab$ | $3a^9$ |
| $a^9b^{11}c^5$ | $-32a^{10}b^{15}c^{40}$ | $1/4\ a^2b^2c^8$ | $a^6b^7c^7$ | $a\ b^2c^6$ | $5a^4$ |
| $1/2a^5b^5$ | $12a^8b^{11}c^{16}$ | $24a^7b^{15}c^8$ | $-1/2a^5b^6$ | $a^4bc^6$ | $a\ b^3c$ |
| $ab^3c$ | $54a^0b^{11}c$ | $108a^7b^4$ | $10a^7b^{13}c^9$ | $a^8b^4$ | $1/32a^5b^5c^6$ |

# Laws of Exponents 3

Name _____     Date _____

**Directions**: Use the designated colors to match the flowers with the correct answers in the boxes below. Write the number of each problem on the lines below each correct answer.

| 1. | 2. | 3. | 4. | 5. | 6. |
|----|----|----|----|----|----|
| Red | Blue | Red | Red | Yellow | Yellow |
| $3^3$ | $3^{-3}$ | $(1/4)^{-3}$ | $(½)^3$ | $(-3)^4$ | $(-5)^{-3}$ |

| 7. | 8. | 9. | 10. | 11. | 12. |
|----|----|----|----|----|----|
| Yellow | Yellow | Blue | Blue | Blue | Blue |
| $10^0$ | $(2/3)^{-2}$ | $10^4$ | $1^{1000}$ | $10^3$ | $(4/2)^3$ |

| 13. | 14. | 15. | 16. | 17. | 18. |
|----|----|----|----|----|----|
| Green | Green | Green | Green | Green | Black |
| $(-2)^{-4}$ | $(2\ 1/3)^3$ | $4^3/4^{-2}$ | $(2^3 3^{-2}$ | $(4^{-2}/4^3)$ | $2^8 3^4/2^6 3^5$ |

| 1/8 | 27 | 81 | 1 1/3 | 8/9 | -1/125 | 2.25 | 1/27 | 1 |
|-----|-----|-----|-----|-----|-----|-----|-----|-----|
| ___ | ___ | ___ | ___ | ___ | ___ | ___ | ___ | ___ |

| 1000 | 10,000 | 64 | 1/16 | 1024 | 12.7 | 8 | 1 | $1/4^5$ |
|------|--------|-----|------|------|------|-----|-----|---------|
| ___ | ___ | ___ | ___ | ___ | ___ | ___ | ___ | ___ |

93

# Laws of Exponents 4

Name _____    Date _____

**Directions**: Solve each problem. Find the answers to the problems in the boxes below. Place the correct letters on the lines under the problems.

**1.** $(2a^2)^2$

_____

**2.** $(-3a^1)^3$

_____

**3.** $(3a^2)^4$

_____

**4.** $(2a^3)^2$

_____

**5.** $(4a^3)^3$

_____

**6.** $(3a^3)^5$

_____

**7.** $(2a^3)^3$

_____

**8.** $(-8a^3)^4$

_____

**9.** $(-2a^3)^5$

_____

**10.** $(2a^5)^5$

_____

**11.** $(-3a^2)^2(a^2)^3$

_____

**12.** $(2a^3)^4$

_____

**13.** $(3a)^2$

_____

**14.** $(-3a^2)^2$

_____

**15.** $(-2a^3)^6(a^4)$

_____

**16.** $(-2a^4)^4$

_____

**17.** $(3a^2)^3a^{10}a^3$

_____

**18.** $(2^23^3(a^3)^2a$

_____

**19.** $5(2^3)(a^4)^2$

_____

**20.** $3^2a^4$

_____

| A | B | C | D | E | F |
|---|---|---|---|---|---|
| $(16a^{12})$ | $(16a^{16})$ | $-32a^{15}$ | $(81a^8)$ | $64a^{22}$ | $(9a^2)$ |
| **V** | **I** | **J** | **K** | **L** | **G** |
| $32a^{25}$ | $4096a^{12}$ | $3a$ | $27a^{19}$ | $8a^9$ | $64a^{26}$ |
| **N** | **U** | **R** | **S** | **Q** | **T** |
| $64a^9$ | $9a^{10}$ | $3a^2$ | $4a^4$ | $108a^7$ | $243a^{15}$ |
| **H** | **O** | **P** | **X** | **Y** | **Z** |
| $9a^4$ | $-17a^3$ | $-27a^3$ | $243a^6$ | $40a^8$ | $4a^6$ |

94

# Laws of Exponents 5

Name _____   Date _____

**Directions**: Use the laws of exponents to solve the problems. Connect these points to form a figure. Connect the answers together.

1. $A^1A^2$

2. $A^2A^4$

3. $A^5A^6$

4. $A^7A^4$

5. $A^{10}A^7$

6. $A^8 A^6$

7. $A^7A^5$

8. $A^3A^8$

9. $A^6A^{-4}$

10. $A^{-4}A^{-3}$

11. $A^{30}A^{-24}$

12. $A^{29}A^{-41}$

13. $A^8A^{-9}$

14. $A^4A^5$

15. $A^{16}A^{-4}$

16. $A^6A^3A^{-4}$

17. $A^{-3}A^8A^{-2}$

18. $A^8A^{-10}A^5$

19. $A^6A^{-5}A^{-7}$

20. $A^8A^9A^{-12}$

21. $A^2A^4A^6$

22. $A^2A^2A^{-8}$

23. $A^5A^{-7}A^6$

24. $A^3A^6A^9$

25. $A^1A^2A^3$

26. $A^7A^{-6}A^8$

27. $A^4A^7$

28. $A^6A^9$

29. $A^8A^9$

30. $A^{-4}A^5A^2$

$A^6 \quad A^{11} \quad A^{11} \quad A^{17} \quad A^{76} \quad A^{-32}$

$A^{20} \qquad A^1 \quad A^{14}$

$A^3A^{-7} \quad A^2 \quad A^{11} \quad A^{12} A^4 A^3$

$A^6 \ A^{17} \ A^{15} \ A^{11} \quad A^9 \ A^6 \ A^{18} \ A^{-4} \ A^{-84}$

$A^9 \qquad A^3 \qquad A^{12}$

$A^{-12} \qquad A^{12} \qquad A^3 \quad A^5 \quad A^{21}$

$A^{16} \ A^9 \ A^{-1} \quad A^5 \qquad A^{-6} \ A^9 \ A^{54}$

$A^{10} \qquad A^{12} \qquad A^{12} \quad A^6$

# Laws of Exponents 6

**Name** _____     **Date** _____

**Directions**: Find the number of yards hit by each person a = -2, b = 2, y = -1, c = 1, x = -1, e = -1, d = 2.

**1.** Alice _____ yds.     **2.** Sarah _____ yds.     **3.** Al _____ yds.

**4.** Mark _____ yds.     **5.** Red _____ yds.     **6.** Mel _____ yds.

**7.** Lou _____ yds.     **8.** Cat _____ yds.     **9.** Ned _____ yds.

**10.** Will _____ yds.     **11.** Me _____ yds.     **12.** Bill _____ yds.

| **Alice** | **Sarah** | **Al** | **Mark** |
|---|---|---|---|
| $Y^6 \, Y^8$ | $(3X^3y^2)(-2X^5Y^5)$ | $(5a^2b^3c^{-2})^1$ | $(2a^2)^3 + -4a^6$ |

| **Red** | **Mel** | **Lou** |
|---|---|---|
| $(8Y^6) \div (4Y^{20})$ | $(8Y^{27}) \div (4Y^{13})$ | $(-7 \, a^{-2}b^5c^6) \div (49 \, a^{-4}b^4 \, c^6)$ |

| **Cat** | **Ned** | **Ted** |
|---|---|---|
| $2a^2(3d)^2$ | $(2ad)^4 \div (2bc)^2$ | $(12 \, a^{-6}) \div (18 \, a^{-7})$ |

| **Will** | **Me** | **Bill** |
|---|---|---|
| $(3c^3(^-b^3)^2$ | $3X^2(2X^3 - 3X^{-2} + 7)$ | $(3X^3 + 7X^2 - 4) - (2X^3 - 5X^2 + 10)$ |

# Laws of Exponents 7

**Name** _____    **Date** _____

**Directions**: Multiply or divide these exponents. Color each box as indicated. Some of the answers are not in the box .Place the answers under the problems.

| **1. Red** | **2. Yellow** | **3. Orange** | **4. Green** | **5. Tan** | **6. Black** |
|---|---|---|---|---|---|
| $a^6/a^4$ | $a^6b^4/a^3b^2$ | $a^3b^4/a^6b^7$ | $(ab)^3/(ab)$ | $a^3b^4/a^6b^8$ | $a^6b^7/ab^4$ |

| **7. Blue** | **8. Brown** | **9. Gray** | **10. Pink** | **11. Red** | **12. Purple** |
|---|---|---|---|---|---|
| $a^5b^7/a^3b^4$ | $(a^2b)(a^4b^3)$ | $2^3/2^2$ | $3^4/3^{-2}$ | $(2y)^4/(2y)^2$ | $4x^7/2x^{-3}$ |

| **13. Red** | **14. Yellow** | **15. Orange** | **16. Green** | **17. Tan** | **18. Black** |
|---|---|---|---|---|---|
| $3X^{-6}/6X^{-3}$ | $(a^3b^2)(a^4b^3)$ | $(a^3b^2)(a^4b^6)^2$ | $(a^6b^4a^{-2}b^{-3})$ | $(a^2b^3)(a^2b^3)(a^2b^3)^2$ | $2(2X)^{-4}/2(6X)^{-4}$ |

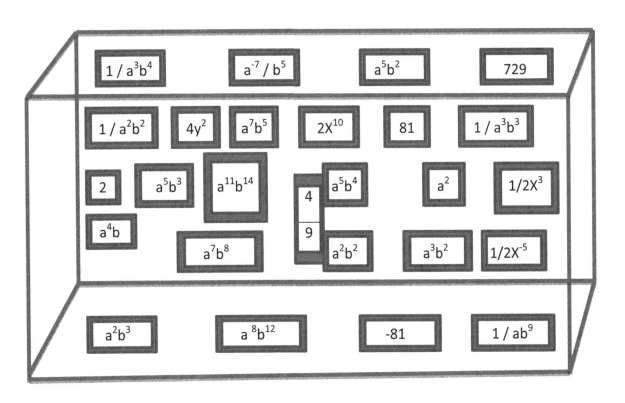

# Scientific Notations 1

Name _____     Date _____

**Directions**: Find the distances from W to B; B to D; F to H; H to K; K to M; M to O; I to P; and B to I. Place the answers on the lines below.

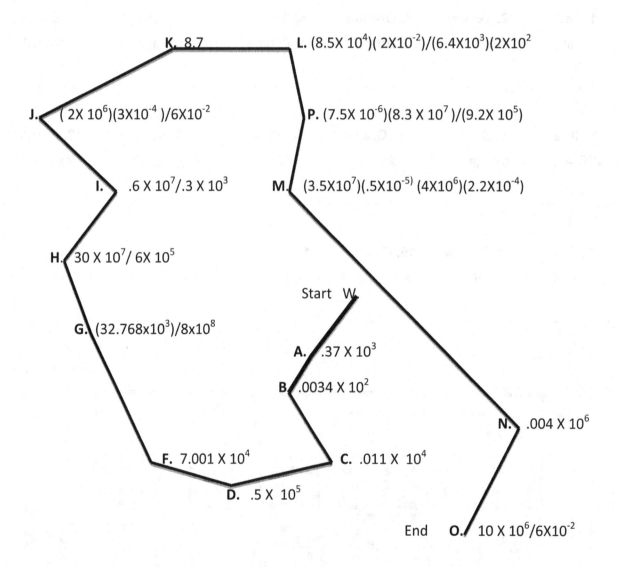

K. 8.7

L. $(8.5 \times 10^4)( 2 \times 10^{-2})/(6.4 \times 10^3)(2 \times 10^2$

J. $( 2 \times 10^6)(3 \times 10^{-4} )/6 \times 10^{-2}$

P. $(7.5 \times 10^{-6})(8.3 \times 10^7 )/(9.2 \times 10^5)$

I. $.6 \times 10^7/.3 \times 10^3$

M. $(3.5 \times 10^7)(.5 \times 10^{-5)} (4 \times 10^6)(2.2 \times 10^{-4})$

H. $30 \times 10^7/ 6 \times 10^5$

Start W

G. $(32.768 \times 10^3)/8 \times 10^8$

A. $.37 \times 10^3$

B. $.0034 \times 10^2$

N. $.004 \times 10^6$

F. $7.001 \times 10^4$

C. $.011 \times 10^4$

D. $.5 \times 10^5$

End   O. $10 \times 10^6/6 \times 10^{-2}$

**1.** W to B _____     **2.** B to D _____     **3.** F to H _____     **4.** H to K _____

**5.** K to M _____     **6.** M to O _____     **7.** I to P _____     **8.** B to I _____

# Scientific Notations 2

Name _____     Date _____

**Directions**: Find the cost of each item. Place the answers on the lines below.

| 1. Ring | 2. Hat | 3. Box | 4. cube | 5. Eye Glasses |
|---------|--------|--------|---------|----------------|
| $ 9.9 X 10^7$ | $ 23333 X10^{-3}$ | $ .54 X 10^3$ | $ 156 X 10^4$ | $ .544 X 10^{-3}$ |

| 6. Watch | 7. Eye | 8. Vase | 9. Shoe | 10. Truck |
|----------|--------|---------|---------|-----------|
| $ 345 X 10^5$ | $ 453 X 10^3$ | $ 30 X 10^2$ | $ . 45 X 10^3$ | $ 1590 X 10^3$ |

| 11. Car | 12. Cup | 13. Bottle | 14. Star | 15. Arrow |
|---------|---------|------------|----------|-----------|
| $ 987 X 10^6$ | $ 7 X 10^3$ | $ 2 X 10^{-2}$ | $ 675.6 X 10^{-2}$ | $ 1000 X 10^{-3}$ |

1. $ _____     2. $ _____     3. $ _____

4. $ _____     5. $ _____     6. $ _____

7. $ _____     8. $ _____     9. $ _____

10. $ _____     11. $ _____     12. $ _____

13. $ _____     14. $ _____     15. $ _____

# Prime Factorization Numbers and Variables 1

Name _____     Date _____

**Directions**: Find the prime factorization for each problem.

| |
|---|
| **1.** $8a^2b^3$ |
| **2.** $15ab^4$ |
| **3.** $20\ a^3b^2$ |
| **4.** $24\ a^3\ b^6$ |
| **5.** $28\ a^2b^2$ |
| **6.** $36a^2b^3$ |
| **7.** $42a^3b^2$ |
| **8.** $48ab$ |
| **9.** $121\ a^6b^5$ |
| **10.** $125ab$ |
| **11.** $175a^4b^4$ |
| **12.** $27b^0$ |
| **13.** $64ab^0$ |
| **14.** $81a^2b^5$ |
| **15.** $56a^0b^0$ |
| **16.** $66a^3b^0$ |
| **17.** $120\ a^5b$ |
| **18.** $50a^3b^4$ |
| **19.** $128\ a\ b^5$ |
| **20.** $72a^4b^3$ |

# Prime Factorizations 2

**Name** _____  **Date** _____

**Directions**: Complete these boxes by finding the correct prime factorizations. Place the answers on the lines in front of the problems.

_____ 1.  $720\ a^5b^4$

K  1x2x2x5x2x5x2aaaaabbb

_____ 2.  $128a^4b^5$

L  1x5x5x3x5x2abbbb

_____ 3.  $160\ a^3b^2$

A  1x3x2x2x2x3x2aaaaabbb

_____ 4.  $648a^4b^2$

B  1X2x2x2x2x2x5aaabb

_____ 5.  $400a^5b^3$

C  1x2x2x2x2x2x2x2aaaabbbb

_____ 6.  $750ab^4$

D  1x2x2x2x3x3x5x2aaaaabbbb

_____ 7.  $350a^3b^6$

E  1x2x2x2x3x3x3x3aaaabb

_____ 8.  $1000ab^6$

F  1x7x5x2x5aaabbbbbb

_____ 9.  $144a^5b^3$

G  1x2x5x2x5x2x5abbbbbb

_____ 10.  $548a^4b^6$

H  1x2x2x137aaaabbbbbb

101

# Prime Factorizations 3

Name _____ Date _____

**Directions**: Find the prime factored form for each number with a color beside it. Each box has a prime factored form in it. Place the correct color over the correct box or beside it.

**1.** 160  Red   **2.** -3240  Black   **3.** 2520  Pink   **4.** -16  Orange   **5.** 3125  Tan   **6.** 220  Blue

**7.** 150  Brown   **8.** 648  Yellow   **9.** 420  Black   **10.** -280  Tan   **11.** 148  Yellow   **12.** 174  Blue

**13.** -100  Pink   **14.** 64  Green   **15.** 363  Tan   **16.** -800  Orange   **17.** 30  Green

| | | | |
|---|---|---|---|
| 1 2 2 2 2 2 3 5 | -1 2 2 2 2 | 1 2 2 2 5 3 3 3 | -1 3 2 11 |
| 1 2 2 37 | 1 3 11 11 | -1 2 2 5 2 7 | 1 2 3 29 |
| -1 2 2 2 5 2 5 2 | 1 3 5 5 2 | 1 2 2 2 3 3 3 3 | -1 5 2 5 2 |
| 1 2 2 2 2 2 | 1 2 11 5 2 | 2 3 5 7 2 | 1 2 3 5 |
| 2 2 2 2 2 2 | 1 5 5 5 5 5 | -5 3 2 2 2 7 3 | 1 2 2 2 2 3 |

102

# Prime Factorizations 4

Name _____ Date _____

**Directions**: Find the factorization for each bottle cap. Match the cap with the correct bottle by placing the letter of the cap on the bottle.

| A | B | C | D | E |
|---|---|---|---|---|
| **1.** ( 16 ) | **2.** ( -32 ) | **3.** ( -54 ) | **4.** ( 162 ) | **5.** ( 770 ) |

| F | G | H | I | J |
|---|---|---|---|---|
| **6.** ( -64 ) | **7.** ( 72 ) | **8.** ( 900 ) | **9.** ( 1540 ) | **10.** ( 18 ) |

| 1 | 1 | -1 | 1 | 1 | -1 | 1 | -1 | 1 | 1 |
|---|---|---|---|---|---|---|---|---|---|
| 3 | 2 | 2 | 2 | 5 | 2 | 3 | 2 | 5 | 3 |
| 3 | 3 | 3 | 2 | 2 | 2 | 3 | 2 | 2 | 3 |
| 2 | 3 | 3 | 2 | 3 | 2 | 2 | 2 | 7 | 2 |
| 2 | 3 | 3 | 2 | 2 | 2 | 2 | 2 | 11 | |
| 3 | 3 | | | 5 | 2 | 2 | 2 | | |
| 5 | | | | 3 | | | | | |

# Greatest Common Factors 1

**Name** _____ **Date** _____

**Directions**: Match the greatest common factor on the left side of the tree with numbers on the right side of the tree. Color the greatest common factor and the two or three numbers the same color.

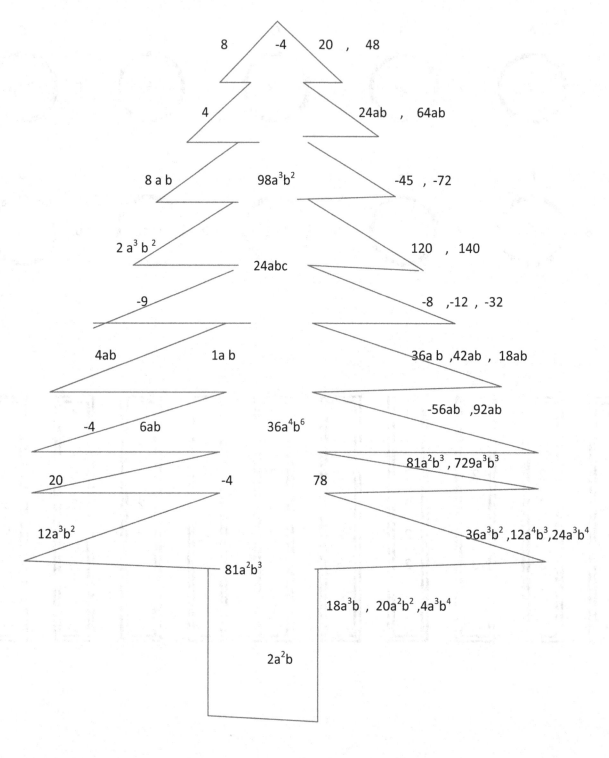

# Greatest Common Factor 2

Name _____     Date _____

**Directions**: The prime factor for each number and variable is given. Color the matching numbers and variables in each set green. Multiply the sets of matches to determine the greatest common factor. Write the greatest common factor on the lines below.

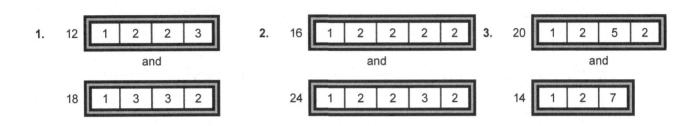

**1.**  12 | 1 | 2 | 2 | 3

and

18 | 1 | 3 | 3 | 2

**2.**  16 | 1 | 2 | 2 | 2 | 2

and

24 | 1 | 2 | 2 | 3 | 2

**3.**  20 | 1 | 2 | 5 | 2

and

14 | 1 | 2 | 7

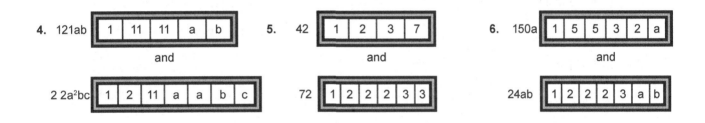

**4.**  121ab | 1 | 11 | 11 | a | b

and

2 2a²bc | 1 | 2 | 11 | a | a | b | c

**5.**  42 | 1 | 2 | 3 | 7

and

72 | 1 | 2 | 2 | 2 | 3 | 3

**6.**  150a | 1 | 5 | 5 | 3 | 2 | a

and

24ab | 1 | 2 | 2 | 2 | 3 | a | b

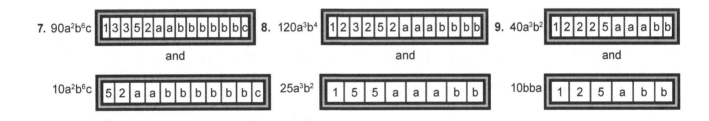

**7.** 90a²b⁶c | 1 | 3 | 3 | 5 | 2 | a | a | b | b | b | b | b | b | c

and

10a²b⁶c | 5 | 2 | a | a | b | b | b | b | b | b | c

**8.** 120a³b⁴ | 1 | 2 | 3 | 2 | 5 | 2 | a | a | a | b | b | b | b

and

25a³b² | 1 | 5 | 5 | a | a | a | b | b

**9.** 40a³b² | 1 | 2 | 2 | 2 | 5 | a | a | a | b | b

and

10bba | 1 | 2 | 5 | a | b | b

The GCF is 1. _____  2. _____  3. _____  4. _____  5. _____  6. _____  7. _____  8. _____  9. _____

# Greatest Common Factor 3

**Name** _____     **Date** _____

**Directions**: Which two or three arrows hit a given bull's eye? Write the letters under the correct answers for the greatest common factors. Write the other GCFs in the target.

**1.** Find the GCF for A and B.

**2.** Find the GCF for C and D.

**3.** Find the GCF for E and F.

**4.** Find the GCF for G and H.

**5.** Find the GCF for H and I.

**6.** Find the GCF for B and F.

**7.** Find the GCF for E and G.

**8.** Find the GCF for D and I.

**9.** Find the GCF for A, B, and C.

**10.** Find the GCF for C, D, and E.

**11.** Find the GCF for F, G , and H.

**12.** Find the GCF for A ,B, and H.

**13.** Find the GCF for E, G, and F.

**14.** Find the GCF for D, H, and A.

**15.** Find the GCF for E, G, and D.

**16.** Find the GCF for F, B, and H.

**17.** Find the GCF for A, H, and B.

| | |
|---|---|
| **A** | 1x2x2x3x2x5 |
| **B** | -1x2x2x2x3x5x7 |
| **C** | 1x3x3x3 |
| **D** | -1x5x2x3x7 |
| **E** | -1x2x1 |
| **F** | 1x2x3x5x7x11 |
| **G** | -1x3x7x11x1 |
| **H** | -1x2x3x2x3x7x1 |
| **I** | -1x5x11x3x13 |

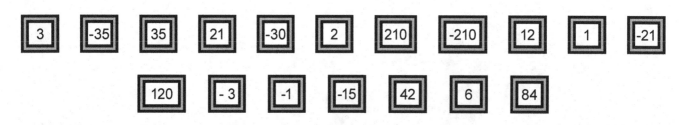

| 3 | -35 | 35 | 21 | -30 | 2 | 210 | -210 | 12 | 1 | -21 |
|---|---|---|---|---|---|---|---|---|---|---|

| 120 | - 3 | -1 | -15 | 42 | 6 | 84 |
|---|---|---|---|---|---|---|

# Greatest Common Factor 4

Name _____    Date _____

**Directions**: Find the greatest common factor for the numbers and variables. Place the answers on the lines below. Show your work.

**(1).**   100    and    92

**(2).**   -112    and    64

**(3).**   25    and    600

**(4).**   10  ,  -4  and  -6

**(5).**   7    and    15

**(6).**   98    and    192

**(7).**   $70a^3b$    and    $28a^2b^2$

**(8).**   $-30a^3b^4$  and  $-48a^3 b^3$

**(9).**   $10a^3b^2$  and  $30a^4b^5$

**(10).**   $b^3$    and    $a^2b^3$

**(11.)**   $12a^3b^4$  and  $18b^6b^2$

**(12.)**   250  and  800

A._____    B._____    C._____    D._____    E._____    F._____

G._____    H._____    I._____    J._____    K._____    L._____

107

# Greatest Common Factor 5

Name _____     Date _____

**Directions**: Find the greatest common factor for the number and variables. Color the answers in the given boxes.

| Red | Orange | Black | Green |
|---|---|---|---|
| **1.** (2x2x2x3x5x7) | **2.** (2x3x2) | **3.** (2x3x7x11x13) | **4.** (1x3x3x2x7x11x3x2x17) |
| (3x7x11x2) | (3x3x2x3x7) | (3x7x11x2) | (1x2x2x3x3) |
| _____ | _____ | _____ | _____ |

| Yellow | Tan | Pink | Brown |
|---|---|---|---|
| **5.** (7x2x3x2x11x3) | **6.** -16 ,-52, and -30 | **7.** 52 and 84 | **8.** 98 and 242 |
| (1x2x3x2x2x11x3) | | | |
| _____ | _____ | _____ | _____ |

| Red | Yellow | Green | Blue |
|---|---|---|---|
| **9.** 72 and 120 | **10.** 75 and 120 | **11.** 75 and 500 | **12.** 37 and 48 |
| _____ | _____ | _____ | _____ |

| 6 | 12 | 25 | -6 | 1 | -3 | 24 | 462 | 36 | 15 | 81 |
|---|---|---|---|---|---|---|---|---|---|---|
| 95 | 594 | 20 | 4 | -5 | 24 | 18 | 42 | 79 | 792 | 12 |
| 34 | 2 | 65 | 396 | -2 | 36 | 6 | 10 | 50 | -4 | 94 |

# Greatest Common Factors 6

**Name** _____ **Date** _____

**Directions**: Find the greatest common factor and place the letters of the answers on the number line.

**A.** (1x2x2) and (1x2x2x3)

**B.** (1x2x2x3) and (1x2x2x3x2)

**C.** (1x3x2 ) and (1x3x2x5)

**D.** (-1x2x3x3x2x3) and (-1x2x3x2)

**E.** (1x2x3x3x3x5x2) and (1x2x3x3x3x7)

**F.** (-1x2x3x5x7x11) and (2x11)

**G.** (1x3x3x2x13) and (1x5x5x13)

**I.** (1x2x2x3x5x2) and (1x3x2x7x2x2)

**H.** (1x3x3x3) and (1x2x5x2x3)

**J.** (1x3x2x5) and (3x5)

**O.** (1x2x3x2x2x5x87) and (1x2x5x3)

**K.** (1x3x3) and (1x3x3x3x3)

**M.** (-1x2x3x5x3) and (1x2x3x7)

**N.** (1x2x2x3x2x3x2x3x2x1x2) and (1x2x3x2x7x2x3)

**L.** (3x5x7) and (7x7x13)

-10  -5  0  5  10  15  20  25  30  35  40  45  50  55  60  70  80

109

# Greatest Common Factor 7

Name _____     Date _____

**Directions**: Find the greatest common factor using letters and symbols.

**1.** ABC + CDAB = _____

**2.** ABCD + ABC + DEAR = _____

**3.** ABC + CDAB + DABCE + ABCD = _____

**4.** ABC + DCAB + ABDEC + DEFABC = _____

**5.** ▢▢◯◯ = _____

**6.** XXXXXXX + XXXXXX + XXXXXX + XXXX = _____

**7.** NUNN + NUNNN + NUNNU = _____

**8.** XUX + XUXXUX + XUXXX + XUX = _____

**9.** 111111 + 1111111 + 111111111 = _____

**Create three greatest common factor examples.**

**10.** _____

**11.** _____

**12.** _____

# Chapter 5

## Multiplying Sums of Squares and Factoring

# Multiplying Sums of Squares

Name _____     Date _____

**Directions**: Multiply these sums or differences of squares. Place answers on your own paper.

1. $(a + b)^2$

2. $(a + c)^2$

3. $(a - b)^2$

4. $(a + b)^2$

5. $(2a - b)^2$

6. $(3c + 2B)^2$

7. $(2a^2 - 3c)^2$

8. $(4a - b)^2$

9. $(-2a + 3b)^2$

10. $(4a^2 + 2b)^2$

11. $(a^2 + 4b)^2$

12. $(b^2 - b^2)^2$

13. $(a + 2c)^2$

14. $(ab + b)^2$

15. $(a^2b^2 - a^2b^2)^2$

16. $(c + b)^2$

17. $(a - c)^2$

18. $(b - a)^2$

19. $(3a + 2b)^2$

20. $(3b + 4a)^2$

# Sum and Difference of Two Cubes

Name _____ Date _____

**Directions**: Match the sums and differences with the answers on the right side.

_____ 1. $X^3 - 1$

_____ 2. $X^3 + 1$

_____ 3. $X^3 - 8$

_____ 4. $8X^3 + 8$

_____ 5. $2X^3 - 16$

_____ 6. $X^3Y^3 - 1$

_____ 7. $X^3Y^3 + 1$

_____ 8. $8X^3 - 8$

_____ 9. $27X^3 - 8$

_____ 10. $X^6 - 1$

_____ 11. $8 - X^3$

_____ 12. $1 - X^3$

_____ 13. $1 + X^3$

**A.** $(X - 1)(x^2 + 2x + 1)(x + 1)(x^2 - 2x + 1)$

**B.** $(XY-1)(X^2Y^2 + XY + 1)$

**C.** $(X - 1)(X^2 + X + 1)$

**D.** $(X - 1)(X^2 + X + 1)$

**E.** $(3X - 2)(9X^2 + 6X + 4)$

**F.** $8(X + 2)(X^2 - 2X + 4)$

**G.** $(X + 1)(X^2 - X + 1)$

**H.** $(X - 1)(X^2 + X + 1)$

**I.** $8(X - 1)(X^2 + X + 1)$

**J.** $2(X - 2)(X^2 + 2X + 4)$

**K.** $Y^3(X + Y)(X^2 - XY + Y^2)$

**L.** $(1 - X)(1 + X + X^2)$

**M.** $(1 + X)(1 - X + X^2)$

**N.** $8(X + 1)(X^2 - X + 1)$

**0.** $(XY + 1)(X^2Y^2 - XY + 1)$

**P.** $(X - 1)(X^2 + X + 1)$

**Q.** $(X + 1)(X^2 - X + 1)$

**R.** $(2 - X)(4 + 2X + X^2)$

# Trinomials 1

Name _____     Date _____

**Directions**: Factor each problem on the left. Place the answers on the right. Use rational numbers. Some answers are not given.

1. $24X^2 - 64X - 10$

2. $21X^2 - 17X + 2$

3. $X^2 - 2X + 8$

4. $2X^2 - 12X - 18$

5. $3X^2 + 2X - 8$

6. $X^2 + 5x + 6$

7. $X^2 + 6X + 5$

8. $X^2 + 2X + 1$

9. $3X^2 - 11X - 4$

10. $36X^2 - 6X - 2$

11. $3X^2 - X - 4$

12. $6X^2 + X - 12$

13. $21X^2 - 14X - 1$

1. _____

2. _____

3. _____

4. _____

5. _____

6. _____

7. _____

8. _____

9. _____

10. _____

11. _____

12. _____

13. _____

# Trinomials 2

**Directions**: Factor these trinomials in the form of a V at the bottom of the page. Place the letters of the answers under the problems.

**A.**  $(3x - 2)(2X + 1)$    **B.**  $(X + 18)(X - 1)$    **C.**  $(2X + 3)(X + 2)$    **D.**  $(3x + 2)(X - 5)$

**E.**  $(x + 1)(X + 18)$    **F.**  $(X - 1)(X - 1)$    **G.**  $(X + 2)(X + 7)$    **H.**  $(3X - 2)(3X - 2)$

**I.**  $(3X - 2)(2X + 1)$    **J.**  $4(X - 3)(X - 1)$    **K.**  $(X + 6)(X - 3)$    **P.**  $(X - 7)(X + 7)$

**M.**  $(2X + 3)(X - 2)$    **N.**  $(2X + 1)(X - 2)$    **L.**  $(2X - 2)(3X - 2)$    **Y.**  (Cannot be factored)

**T.**  $(x + 1)(X + 2)$    **U.**  $(74)(5X)$    **V.**  $(X + 4)(X + 1)$    **W.**  $(2X - 3)(2X + 1)$

**X.**  $(2X + 3)(2X - 1)$    **Q.**  $(3X + 2)(3x + 2)$    **S.**  $(X - 2)(X + 2)$    **Z.**  $(3X + 2)(2X - 1)$

**1.** $9X^2 - 12X + 4$                                         **7.** $X^2 + 3X + 2$

_____                                                         _____

**2.** $4X^2 + 4X - 3$                                          **8.** $6X^2 - X - 2$

_____                                                         _____

**3.** $6X^2 - X - 2$                                            **9.** $X^2 + 19X + 18$

_____                                                         _____

**4.** $3X^2 - 13X - 10$                                        **10.** $2X^2 + 7X + 6$

_____                                                         _____

**5.** $9X^2 + 12X + 4$                                         **11.** $4X^2 - 4X - 3$

_____                                                         _____

**6.** $X^2 - 2X + 1$                                            **12.** $4X^2 - 16X + 12$

_____                                                         _____

**13.** $X^2 - 4$

_____

# Trinomials 3

Name _____     Date _____

**Directions**: Find the number by factoring the trinomials in the correct order. Write the number of the correct answer in the space provided at the bottom of the page.

**1.** $12X^2 + 5X - 3$

**2.** $5X^2 + 9X - 2$

**3.** $12X^2 - 5X - 3$

**4.** $5X^2 + 11X + 2$

**5.** $4X^2 + 4X - 3$

**6.** $X^2 - 6X + 9$

**7.** $X^2 - 9X + 20$

**8.** $X^2 + 6X + 9$

**9.** $2X^2 - X - 6$

**10.** $2X^2 + 5X - 3$

**11.** $X^2 - 2X + 1$

**12.** $2X^2 - 5X - 3$

**13.** $5X^2 - 9X - 2$

**14.** $12X^2 + 13X + 3$

**15.** $2X^2 + 5X - 3$

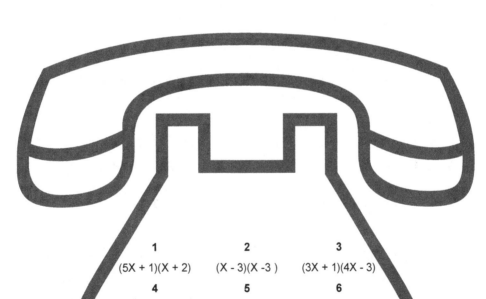

| 1 | 2 | 3 |
|---|---|---|
| $(5X + 1)(X + 2)$ | $(X - 3)(X - 3)$ | $(3X + 1)(4X - 3)$ |
| **4** | **5** | **6** |
| $(3X + 1)(4X + 3)$ | $(5X - 1)(X + 2)$ | $(2X - 1)(X + 3)$ |
| **7** | **8** | **9** |
| $(2X + 1)(X - 3)$ | $(X + 3)(X + 3)$ | $(3X - 1)(4X + 3)$ |
| | **0** | |
| * | $(5X + 1)(X - 2)$ | # |

# Trinomials 4

**Name** _____     **Date** _____

**Directions**: Factor the trinomials on the tree. Write the numbers of the correct answers below in the proper spaces on the tree. Place the answers on the lines.

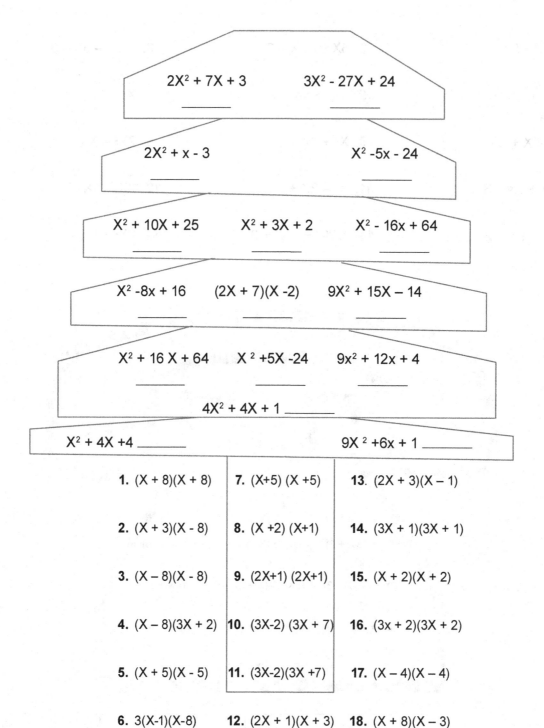

$2X^2 + 7X + 3$ _____     $3X^2 - 27X + 24$ _____

$2X^2 + x - 3$ _____     $X^2 - 5x - 24$ _____

$X^2 + 10X + 25$ _____     $X^2 + 3X + 2$ _____     $X^2 - 16x + 64$ _____

$X^2 - 8x + 16$ _____     $(2X + 7)(X - 2)$ _____     $9X^2 + 15X - 14$ _____

$X^2 + 16X + 64$ _____     $X^2 + 5X - 24$ _____     $9x^2 + 12x + 4$ _____

$4X^2 + 4X + 1$ _____

$X^2 + 4X + 4$ _____          $9X^2 + 6x + 1$ _____

**1.** $(X + 8)(X + 8)$     **7.** $(X+5)(X +5)$     **13.** $(2X + 3)(X - 1)$

**2.** $(X + 3)(X - 8)$     **8.** $(X +2)(X+1)$     **14.** $(3X + 1)(3X + 1)$

**3.** $(X - 8)(X - 8)$     **9.** $(2X+1)(2X+1)$     **15.** $(X + 2)(X + 2)$

**4.** $(X - 8)(3X + 2)$     **10.** $(3X-2)(3X + 7)$     **16.** $(3x + 2)(3X + 2)$

**5.** $(X + 5)(X - 5)$     **11.** $(3X-2)(3X +7)$     **17.** $(X - 4)(X - 4)$

**6.** $3(X-1)(X-8)$     **12.** $(2X + 1)(X + 3)$     **18.** $(X + 8)(X - 3)$

# Quadratic Equations 1

Name _____     Date _____

**Directions**: Solve the quadratic equations by factoring. Place the letter of the correct answer to the problem in the correct box.

**A.** $X^2 - 4X = 0$

**B.** $X^2 + 6X = 0$

**C.** $X^2 - 4 = 0$

**D.** $8X^2 - 20X = 0$

**E.** $X^2 = 16$

**F.** $X^2 + 2X + 1 = 0$

**G.** $3X^2 + 20X = 0$

**H.** $24X^2 - 61X = -35$

**I.** $1/4X^2 - 2X + 4 = 0$

**J.** $6X^2 + 5X + 1 = 0$

**K.** $X^4 - 36 = 0$

**L.** $6X^2 + 16X = 32$

**M.** $2X^2 - 98 = 0$

**N.** $4X^3 - 100X = 0$

**O.** $X^3 - 2X^2 - 4X + 8 = 0$     **P.** $6X^2 + 19X - 7 = 0$

**Q.** $X^2 + 8X + 12 = 0$

**R.** $X^4 - 13X^2 = -36$

**S.** $X^3 = -5X^2 - 6X$

**T.** $1/4X^2 + X - 8 = 0$

| -7,7,0 | .3,-3 1/2 | 0,3,3, | -8,0,0,0 | 9,9,9,9 | 8,8,8,9 | 9,9,9,9 | 9,9,9,9 | 9,9,9,9 |
|---|---|---|---|---|---|---|---|---|
| -7,7 | 1/3,3 1/2 | 6, 4 | ±2.45,±√-6 | 3,-3,2 | 3 ,3 | -3 ,3 | 7/8,1 2/3 | -8,4 |
| -4,-4 | 7 , 5 | -8 | -1/3,-1/2 | 2 , 2 | 10 | 3 , - 7 | 0 ,-5, 5 | -6,-2 |
| -7 ,6 | 1 , 3 | 9 , 8 | -1 , - 1 | 0 , 2.5 | 11 ,7 | 6 , 2 | 3 , 2 | 0 , 6 |
| 10,-7 | -7/8,-1.7 | 6,2 | -8,-4 | 1/3,.5 | 7 , -7 | -4,1.3 | 6,7,1 | 0,6.67 |
| 5,2 | 3,-3,2.-2 | 30 | 7 , 1 | 8, -4 | 7 | 8 | 0 , 3 , 2 | 1 , 2 |
| 0 ,-25 | 2 ,-2,2 | 0 , - 6 | 0 ,- 6.67 | 3 | -3,-4 | 1 , -4 | -7/8,1.6 | 1 ,6 |
| 1, 7 | -4,-4,1,6 | 6 ,5 | .33,-.5 | 1, 6 | -6 ,-2 | 0 ,4 | 4 , 4 | -4 ,4 |
| 9 ,1 | 0 ,-3 , -2 | 1 , -7 | 0 ,1,-6 | 3 , 2 | 2 , -2 | 1,1,1 | 4 , 0 | -9 , 6 |
| 7,-7 | -1/3,-3.5 | -6,-4 | 3,-3,-2 | -3 ,-3 | -7/8,1 | -8,-1 | -1,-1,-1 | -3 ,-3 |

119

# Quadratic Equations 2

Name _____     Date _____

**Directions** Solve the quadratic equations and place the correct letters under the correct answer.

**A.** $9X^2 - 30X + 4 = 0$

**B.** $4X^2 + X - 3 = 0$

**C.** $3X^2 + X - 10 = 0$

**D.** $X^2 + 16 = 6X$

**E.** $2X^2 + 11X - 51 = 0$

**F.** $X^2 - 98 = 0$

**G.** $X^2 - 3X + 79 = 0$

**H.** $4X^2 - 6X - 42 = 0$

**I.** $X^2 - 10X - 48 = 0$

**J.** $3X^2 + 5X - 3 = 0$

**K.** $4X^2 - 40 = 0$

**L.** $3X^2 - 6X - 7 = 0$

**M.** $2X^3 + 4X^2 - 16X = 0$

**N.** $X^2 - 36 = 0$

**O.** $1/2X^2 - 4X = 0$

0,   .139,   .47,   .75,   1.67,   2,   2.14,   2.83,   3,   3.16,   3.19,   9.90   4.08,   ± 6,   8,   $3 \pm 2.65i$

—   —   —   —   —   —   —   —   —   —   —   —   —   —   ——

-.83,   -1,   -2,   -2.58,   -3.16,   -3.55,   -4,   -8.5,   -2.14,   2,   -9.90,   13.55,   -.709,   $(3\pm17.53)/2$

—   —   —   —   —   —   —   —   —   —   —   —   ——

# Quadratic Equations 3

**Directions**: Find the solution to each quadratic equation. Match the equation with the correct answer below by placing the letter on the line beside the answer.

**A.** $2X^2 - 2X + 2 = 0$     **B.** $X^2 + 9X - 4 = 0$     **C.** $2X^2 + 4X - 3 = 0$     **D.** $X^2 - 3X = 0$

**E.** $3X^2 - 2X + 2 = 0$     **F.** $3X^2 + 4X + 1/2 = 0$     **G.** $1/2X^2 + 4X + 1 = 0$     **H.** $4X^2 - 3X + 2 = 0$

**I.** $X^2 - 9 = 0$     **J.** $X^2 + 3 = 0$     **K.** $1.2X^2 - 4X - 1 = 0$     **L.** $X^2 - 12 = 0$

**M.** $X^2 - \frac{1}{2} = 0$     **N.** $5X^2 - 10X = 0$     **O.** $X^2 + 6X = 0$     **P.** $X^2 + 32X = 0$

**Q.** $4X^2 - 3X + 6 = 0$     **R.** $4X^2 - 2X = 0$     **S.** $X^2 - 25 = 0$

.±5 _____          $X = 1/2, X = 0.$ _____          $.(1 \pm i\sqrt{3})/2$ _____

$(3 \pm i\sqrt{87})/8.$ _____          $.(-9 \pm \sqrt{97})/2$ _____

$X = 0, X = -32.$ _____     $.x = 0, x = -6$ _____          $.(-2 \pm \sqrt{10})/2$ _____

$.\pm \sqrt{2}/2$ _____          $X = 0, X = 2.$ _____

$.X = 0, X = 3$ _____     $.\pm 2\sqrt{3}$ _____          $X = 3, X = -3.$ _____

$(1 \pm i\sqrt{5})/3$ _____     $(3 \pm i\sqrt{23})/8$ _____          $\pm i\sqrt{3}.$ _____

$-4 \pm \sqrt{10})/6$ _____          $.(4 \pm \sqrt{20.8})/2.4$ _____

$-4 \pm \sqrt{14}$ _____     $\pm \sqrt{2}/2.$ _____          $.X = 0, X = 2$ _____

121

# Quadratic Equations 4

Name _____     Date _____

**Directions**: Write Yes or No to indicate if the quadratic equation is in the correct box. Use the discriminant ($b^2 - 4ac$) to find the solutions.

| | | |
|---|---|---|
| **1 Rational** | $X^2 -4X -3 = 0$ _____ | $X^2 - 25 = 0$ _____ |
| **1 solution** | $2X^2 -4X + 2 = 0$ _____ | $X^2 + 64 = 0$ _____ |
| | $7X^2 +5X +3 = 0$ _____ | $8X^2 - 8X + 2 = 0$ _____ |

| | |
|---|---|
| **Not a perfect square** | $X^2 -4X = 0$ _____ |
| **Perfect square** | $5X^2 -3x + 9 =$ _____ |
| **2 real numbers** | $2X^2 - 3X +1 = 0$ _____ |
| **Irrational numbers** | $4X^2 -36 = 0$ _____ |
| **2 Rational** | $5X^2 + 3X + 9 = 0$ _____ |
| **Unequal numbers** | $3X^2 -6X = 0$ _____ |

| | | |
|---|---|---|
| **No real number** | $X^2 -10X + 25 = 0$ _____ | $5X^2 - 10X + 3 = 0$ _____ |
| **Different roots** | $4X^2 -6X + 3 = 0$ _____ | $X^2 -3X + 4 = 0$ _____ |
| **No solution** | $X^2 -2X -1 = 0$ _____ | |
| **2 complex conjugate** | $4X^2 -49 = 0$ _____ | |

# Chapter 6

## Radical Equations

# Divisibility Rules 1

**Directions**: Study the divisibility rules below.

A number is divisible by 2, if the last digit is even. 22, 64 , 90 ; 656, 300, and 28

A number is divisible by 3, if the sum of the digit is divisible by 3. 306, 11, 112.

A number is divisible by 4, if the last 2 digits are divisible by 4. 124, 3212, 88.

A number is divisible by 5, if the last digits is 0 or 5. 55, 380 ; 4,000, 0005.

A number is divisible by 6, if the number is divisible by both 2 and 3. 1008.

A number is divisible by 8, if the last digits are divisible by 8. 109, 816

A number is divisible by 9, if the sum of the digits is divisible by 9. 111, 321

A number is divisible by 10, if the number ends in 0. 62, 316, 120

A number is divisible by 12, if the number is divisible by both 3 and 4.

Write Y if a number is divisible by 2, 3, 4, 5, 6, 8, 9, 10, and 12.

Write N if a number is not divisible by 2, 3, 4, 5, 6, 8, 9, 10, and 12.

| Number | 2 | 3 | 4 | 5 | 6 | 8 | 9 | 10 | 12 |
|---------|---|---|---|---|---|---|---|----|----|
| 231 | | | | | | | | | |
| 505 | | | | | | | | | |
| 3291 | | | | | | | | | |
| 12,870 | | | | | | | | | |
| 54,322 | | | | | | | | | |
| 3000024 | | | | | | | | | |
| 54 | | | | | | | | | |

# Perfect Square Roots 2

Name _____ Date _____

**Directions**: Find the perfect squares of these numbers. Place the letter under the correct answer in the boxes. Some answers are not given.

**A.** √4    **B.** √9    **C.** √121    **D.** √484    **E.** √36    **F.** √256    **G.** √1600

**H.** √100    **I.** √441    **J.** √25    **K.** √400    **L.** √81    **M.** √169    **N.** √16

**O.** √1225    **P.** √324    **Q.** √64    **R.** √196    **S.** √289    **T.** √49    **U.** √625

| 2 | 31 | 104 | 3 | 37 | 40 | 50 | 12 | 61 | 123 |
|---|---|---|---|---|---|---|---|---|---|
| 63 | 49 | 25 | 12 | 21 | -65 | 17 | -85 | 9 | -54 |
| 38 | 72 | 97 | 22 | 83 | 67 | 200 | 35 | -53 | 10 |
| 94 | 20 | 87 | 67 | 69 | 39 | 7 | -65 | 111 | 196 |
| 1 | 56 | 42 | 11 | 75 | 14 | 74 | 5 | 105 | 7 |
| 6 | 24 | 8 | 144 | 61 | 18 | 103 | 83 | 16 | 195 |

# Square Roots 3

Name _____     Date _____

**Directions**: Find the square root of each number and determine which person won the race.
Place an "X" on each correct answer.

_____ is the winner.

**1.** √8     **2.** √18     **3.** √12     **4.** √20     **5.** √28     **6.** √72     **7.** √75

**8.** √44     **9.** √48     **10.** √200     **11.** √84     **12.** √140     **13.** √56     **14.** √21

**15.** √150     **16.** √92     **17.** √126     **18.** √80     **19.** √2     **20.** √27     **21.** √300

| JACK | RED | MARY |
|------|-----|------|
| 4 √5 | 5 √2 | 2 √14 |
| 5 √3 | 2 √7 | 3 √2 |
| √21 | 4 √3 | 6 √2 |
| 2 √2 | 4 √5 | √21 |
| 2 √17 | 2 √5 | 2 √21 |
| 2 √11 | 11 √2 | 3 √5 |
| 5 √6 | 5 √3 | 2 √3 |
| 3 √2 | 3 √14 | 10 √2 |
| 2 √6 | 2 √11 | √8 |

# Square Roots 4

**Name** _____     **Date** _____

**Directions**: Find the square roots of these problems.

**1.** $\sqrt{4a^6b^9c^2}$ = _____

**2.** $\sqrt{4a^2b^4c^6}$ = _____

**3.** $\sqrt{27a^3c^5}$ = _____

**4.** $\sqrt{25a^3}$ = _____

**5.** $\sqrt{18a^2b^7c^8}$ = _____

**6.** $\sqrt{8ab^5c^7}$ = _____

**7.** $\sqrt{80a^7b^9}$ = _____

**8.** $\sqrt{64a^9b^8c^7}$ = _____

**9.** $\sqrt{120a^3b^7c^9d^8}$ = _____

**10.** $\sqrt{228a^3b^6}$ = _____

**11.** $\sqrt{1000a^5}$ = _____

**12.** $\sqrt{250a^7b^5c^{36}}$ = _____

**13.** $\sqrt{336a^{12}b^{13}c^{54}}$ = _____

**14.** $\sqrt{400abc^9}$ = _____

**15.** $\sqrt{81a^2bc^4}$ = _____

# Square Roots 5

Name _____     Date _____

**Directions**: In Column I the square roots are listed. Using Columns II, III, and IV choose one letter to represent a step in finding the square root. List the three steps in the correct order on the lines provided.

| | Column I | Column II | Column III |
|---|---|---|---|
| **1.** √ 28 | **I** <br> √ 10 x 10 x 2 | **A** <br> √ 9 x 2 | **Q** <br> 2 x √ 7 |
| **2.** √ 200 | **J** <br> √ 6 x 6 x 10 | **C** <br> √ 100 x 10 | **R** <br> 7 x √ 2 |
| **3.** √ 18 | **K** <br> √ 2 x 2 x 7 | **D** <br> √ 4 x 2 | **S** <br> 6 x √ 10 |
| **4.** √ 98 | **L** <br> √ 10 x 10 x 10 | **E** <br> √ 49 x 2 | **B** <br> 2 x √ 2 |
| **5.** √ 360 | **N** <br> √ 2 x 2 x 2 | **F** <br> √ 4 x 7 | **U** <br> 3 √ 2 |
| **6.** √ 1000 | **O** <br> √ 3 x 3 x 2 | **G** <br> √ 100 x 2 | **Z** <br> 10 x √ 2 |
| **7.** √ 8 | **P** <br> √ 7 x 7 x 2 | **H** <br> √ 36 x 10 | **T** <br> 10 x √ 10 |

1. _____   2. _____   3. _____   4. _____   5. _____   6. _____   7. _____

# Square Roots 6

Name _____     Date _____

**Directions**: Find the square root of the numbers below. Color the answer in the given quadrant.

| | | | | |
|---|---|---|---|---|
| **1.** $\sqrt{4}$ | **2.** $\sqrt{12}$ | **3.** $\sqrt{8}$ | **4.** $\sqrt{16}$ | **5.** $\sqrt{18}$ |
| **6.** $\sqrt{20}$ | **7.** $\sqrt{24}$ | **8.** $\sqrt{2}$ | **9.** $\sqrt{36}$ | **10.** $\sqrt{80}$ |
| **11.** $\sqrt{45}$ | **12.** $\sqrt{48}$ | **13.** $\sqrt{90}$ | **14.** $\sqrt{120}$ | **15.** $\sqrt{130}$ |
| **16.** $\sqrt{248}$ | **17.** $\sqrt{298}$ | **18.** $\sqrt{625}$ | **19.** $\sqrt{136}$ | **20.** $\sqrt{900}$ |
| **21.** $\sqrt{436}$ | **22.** $\sqrt{964}$ | **23.** $\sqrt{148}$ | **24.** $\sqrt{1114}$ | **25.** $\sqrt{575}$ |

| | | | | | | | | | |
|---|---|---|---|---|---|---|---|---|---|
| $\sqrt{2}$ | 1 | $\sqrt{2}$ | $\sqrt{101}$ | 17 | $\sqrt{31}$ | $2\sqrt{181}$ | $2\sqrt{62}$ | $2\sqrt{34}$ | 4 |
| 1 | $\sqrt{130}$ | $\sqrt{61}$ | $2\sqrt{5}$ | $\sqrt{14}$ | $\sqrt{101}$ | $15\sqrt{2}$ | $\sqrt{11}$ | $2\sqrt{7}$ | $6\sqrt{2}$ |
| $2\sqrt{37}$ | $\sqrt{17}$ | $\sqrt{13}$ | $2\sqrt{34}$ | $3\sqrt{2}$ | $2\sqrt{37}$ | $9\sqrt{10}$ | 6 | 2 | $\sqrt{15}$ |
| $\sqrt{6}$ | $3\sqrt{5}$ | $\sqrt{15}$ | 25 | 50 | $\sqrt{91}$ | 20 | $\sqrt{7}$ | $3\sqrt{2}$ | 12 |
| 4 | $\sqrt{19}$ | $\sqrt{71}$ | $\sqrt{50}$ | $2\sqrt{2}$ | $\sqrt{71}$ | $2\sqrt{2}$ | $2\sqrt{3}$ | 4 | 5 |
| $\sqrt{14}$ | $\sqrt{101}$ | $\sqrt{7}$ | $4\sqrt{2}$ | $\sqrt{50}$ | $3\sqrt{17}$ | 6 | $3\sqrt{2}$ | $\sqrt{30}$ | $\sqrt{29}$ |
| $\sqrt{6}$ | $\sqrt{31}$ | 2 | 4 | $3\sqrt{2}$ | $\sqrt{3}$ | $\sqrt{7}$ | $\sqrt{11}$ | $\sqrt{3}$ | 17 |
| $\sqrt{61}$ | $2\sqrt{34}$ | $\sqrt{91}$ | $\sqrt{2}$ | $3\sqrt{10}$ | $\sqrt{91}$ | $2\sqrt{37}$ | $\sqrt{71}$ | $2\sqrt{2}$ | 9 |
| $5\sqrt{23}$ | $2\sqrt{2}$ | 17 | 11 | $\sqrt{11}$ | $\sqrt{31}$ | $\sqrt{6}$ | $\sqrt{50}$ | $2\sqrt{3}$ | 12 |
| $\sqrt{29}$ | $\sqrt{51}$ | 16 | $2\sqrt{37}$ | 15 | $\sqrt{15}$ | $\sqrt{19}$ | $10\sqrt{10}$ | 4 | $2\sqrt{34}$ |

# Rationalizing the Denominators 7

Name _____     Date _____

**Directions**: Rationalize these denominators. Place the correct letter of the answers on the lines below.

| | | |
|---|---|---|
| **1.** $2/\sqrt{3}$ | **2.** $5/\sqrt{2}$ | |

**A.** $(15 + 5\sqrt{2})/7$   **E.** $(-2\sqrt{5})/15)$   **L.** $(21 - 3\sqrt{3})/46$

| | |
|---|---|
| **3.** $3/2\sqrt{2}$ | **4.** $-2/3\sqrt{5}$ |

**B.** $(4 - 4\sqrt{a})/(1-a)$   **G.** $-1 + \sqrt{2}$   **C.** $-4 + 2\sqrt{3}$

| | |
|---|---|
| **5.** $1/\sqrt{3}$ | **6.** $3/\sqrt{X}$ |

**D.** $(-10 -5\sqrt{b})/4 - b$   **I.** $3\sqrt{2}/4$   **N.** $3\sqrt{X}/X^2$

| | |
|---|---|
| **7.** $1/(1 + \sqrt{2})$ | **8.** $-2/(2 + \sqrt{3})$ |

**H.** $\sqrt{(X)} - X)/(1-X)$   **M.** $2\sqrt{3}/3$   **F.** $5\sqrt{2}/2$

| | |
|---|---|
| **9.** $5/(3 - \sqrt{2})$ | **10.** $-3/(7 - \sqrt{3})$ |

**J.** $\sqrt{3}/3$   **K.** $(-2X\sqrt{X} -X^2)/(4-X)$

| | |
|---|---|
| **11.** $4/(1 + \sqrt{a})$ | **12.** $-5/(2 - \sqrt{b})$ |

**P.** $3\sqrt{X}/X$   **Q.** $(-2X\sqrt{X} - X^2)/(4 - X)$

| | |
|---|---|
| **13.** $\sqrt{X}/(1 + \sqrt{X})$ | **14.** $-X\sqrt{X}/(2 - \sqrt{X})$ |

1. _____   2. _____   3. _____   4. _____   5. _____   6. _____   7. _____

8. _____   9. _____   10. _____   11. _____   12. _____   13. _____   14. _____

131

# Square Roots 8

Name _____     Date _____

**Directions**: Solve each problem and color the correct answers in the squares below. The team with the larger number of correct answers is the winner.

1. $\sqrt{(1/3)}$

2. $\sqrt{(2/9)}$

3. $\sqrt{(4/3)}$

4. $\sqrt{(7/6)}$

5. $\sqrt{(5/6)}$

6. $\sqrt{(14/8)}$

7. $\sqrt{(5/12)}$

8. $\sqrt{(8/9)}$

9. $\sqrt{(2/3)}$

10. $\sqrt{(3/2)}$

11. $\sqrt{(7/4)}$

12. $\sqrt{(2/5)}$

13. $\sqrt{(1/5)}$

14. $\sqrt{(3/5)}$

15. $\sqrt{(1/6)}$

16. $\sqrt{(½)}$

17. $\sqrt{(7/11)}$

18. $\sqrt{(¾)}$

19. $\sqrt{(13/14)}$

20. $\sqrt{42/38}$

### Team A

| √ 6/2 | √ 15/6 | 1/2 |
|-------|--------|-----|
| √ 7/2 | √ 2/3 | √ 15/4 |
| √ 10 | √ 15 | 3/4 |

### Team B

| √ 3/2 | √ 2/5 | √ 10/5 |
|-------|-------|--------|
| √ 5/3 | √ 2/7 | √ 37/6 |
| √ 42/6 | √ 15/5 | √ 8/3 |

# Square Roots 9

**Name** _____  **Date** _____

**Directions**: Add or subtract these square roots. Color the answers in the triangle the designated colors. Write the letter of the problems in the correct space with its answer.

**A.** Red   $+ \sqrt{5} - \sqrt{20}$

**B.** Green   $\sqrt{5} + \sqrt{5}$

**C.** Yellow   $9\sqrt{3} - 3\sqrt{3}$

**D.** Orange   $\sqrt{8} + \sqrt{18}$

**E.** Purple   $\sqrt{1000}$

**F.** Blue   $\sqrt{50} + \sqrt{12}$

**G.** Tan   $\sqrt{72} - \sqrt{28} - \sqrt{128}$

**H.** Brown   $\sqrt{12} + \sqrt{27}$

**I.** Green   $\sqrt{20} - \sqrt{5}$

**J.** Orange   $\sqrt{36} + \sqrt{100} + \sqrt{25}$

**K.** Orange   $\sqrt{15} - \sqrt{60}$

**L.** Red   $3\sqrt{27} - 2\sqrt{48} + \sqrt{80}$

**M.** Green   $\sqrt{128} - \sqrt{32} + \sqrt{98}$

**N.** Purple   $\sqrt{288} - \sqrt{48}$

**O.** Green   $\sqrt{144} - \sqrt{1296} + \sqrt{576}$

**Q.** Yellow   $\sqrt{147} + 2\sqrt{108} - 3\sqrt{27}$

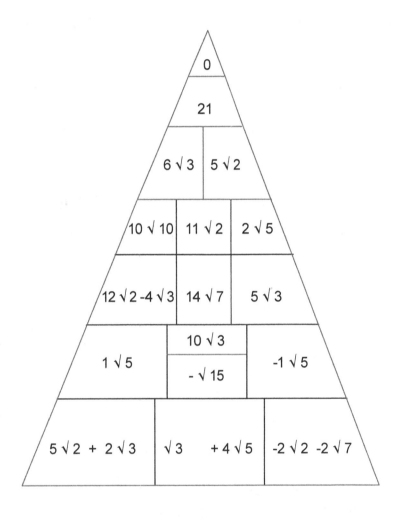

# Square Roots 10

Name _____     Date _____

**Directions**: Multiply each problem and color each part of the car the designated color.

| **1. Black** | **2. Blue** | **3. Red** |
|---|---|---|
| $(\sqrt{3} - 3)(\sqrt{3} + 3)$ | $(3 - \sqrt{3})(3 + \sqrt{3})$ | $(2 - \sqrt{3})(\sqrt{2} + 3)$ |

| **4. Blue** | **5. Gray** | **6. Green** |
|---|---|---|
| $\sqrt{4}(\sqrt{3} + \sqrt{8})$ | $(\sqrt{2} - 2)(\sqrt{2} + 2)$ | $(2 - \sqrt{2})(2 + \sqrt{3})$ |

| **7. Yellow** | **8. Purple** | **9. Orange** |
|---|---|---|
| $(\sqrt{3} + \sqrt{3})(\sqrt{3} + \sqrt{3})$ | $(\sqrt{3} - \sqrt{2})(\sqrt{2} + \sqrt{3})$ | $(3 - \sqrt{3})(\sqrt{5} + 3)$ |

| **10. Red** | **11. Black** | **12. Blue** |
|---|---|---|
| $(\sqrt{8} + \sqrt{6})(5 + \sqrt{18})$ | $(\sqrt{12} - \sqrt{20})(\sqrt{24} + \sqrt{8})$ | $(\sqrt{12} - \sqrt{36})(\sqrt{16} + \sqrt{48})$ |

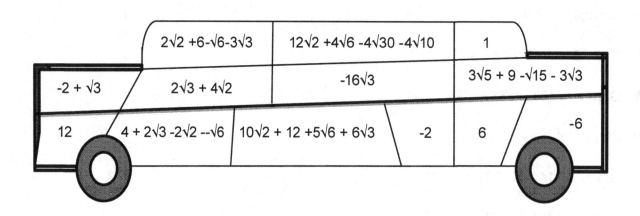

# Radical Equations 11

Name _____     Date _____

**Directions**: Solve the radical equations to determine which part of the remote can be turned on. If the answer is not found on the remote that part can not be turned on. Color the parts of the remote control that can be turned on.

**1.** $\sqrt{2X} = 3$

**2.** $\sqrt{2X} = -18$

**3.** $\sqrt[3]{2X} = 6$

**4.** $\sqrt{2x} + 2 = 8$

**5.** $3\sqrt{2X} + 2 = 4\sqrt{2x} - 7$

**6.** $\sqrt{2X} + 3 = 9$

**7.** $(\sqrt{x} - 3) + 3 = 9$

**8.** $2(\sqrt{x} - 4) \div -4 = 8$

**9.** $(\sqrt{3/5x}) = 5$

**10.** $3\sqrt{X} + 3 = -2\sqrt{x} - 9$

**11.** $(\sqrt{x^2 + 3x + 7}) + 3 = 8$

**12.** $(\sqrt{2x^2 + 3x + 5}) = 3$

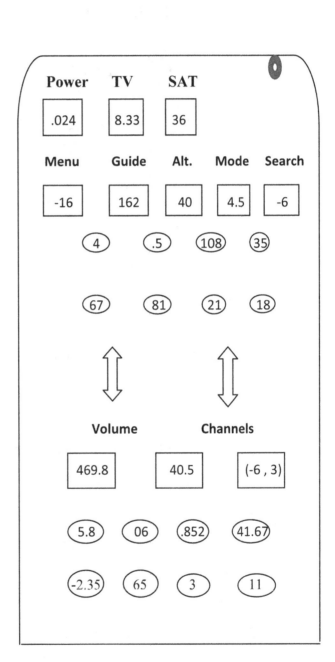

# Radical Equations 12

Name _____     Date _____

**Directions**: Solve the radical equations and place the answers beside the given color. Show your work.

**1.** $\sqrt{(4x + 6)} = x - 2$

**2.** $\sqrt{(2x)} - 1 = 19$

**3.** $3\sqrt{(2x)} + 3 = 4$

**4.** $(x - 2) = \sqrt{x} + 2$

**5.** $X = \sqrt{(2x)} + 3$

**6.** $2\sqrt{(x)} = 20$

**7.** $\sqrt{(2X)} = 4$

**8.** $\sqrt{(2x)} - 1 = 15$

**9.** $\sqrt{(2x)} = 3$

**10.** $\sqrt{(2x/3)} = 4$

**11.** $X = \sqrt{(x)} + 1$

**12.** $2\sqrt{2x} = 8$

_____ Red 8        _____ Red 200        _____ Red 1/18        _____ Red 128

_____ Yellow 100        _____ Yellow 4.5        _____ Yellow 8.24 and -.25        _____ Yellow $(8\pm2\sqrt{7})/2$

_____ Green 16        _____ Green 24        _____ Green $(9\pm\sqrt{17})/2$        _____ Green 2.62 and .38

# Pythagorean Theorem 1

**Name** _____  **Date** _____

**Directions**: Use $A^2 + B^2 = C^2$ to determine the perimeter of the figure.

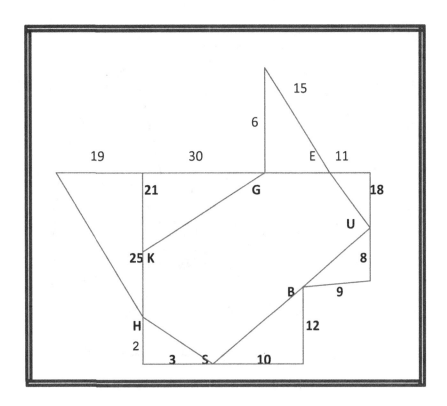

Find   HS _____ SB _____ BU _____ UE _____ EG _____ GK _____ KH _____

# Pythagorean Theorem 2

**Name** _____     **Date** _____

**Directions**: Use $A^2 + B^2 = C^2$ to find the hypotenuse and sides of the right triangle.

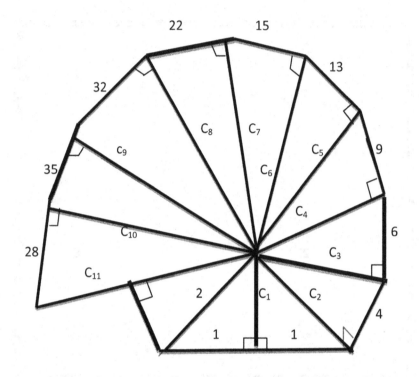

Find   $C_1$ _____ $C_2$ _____ $C_3$ _____ $C_4$ _____ $C_5$ _____

$C_6$ _____ $C_7$ _____ $C_8$ _____ $C_9$ _____ $C_{10}$ _____

# Pythagorean Theorem 3

**Name** _____     **Date** _____

**Directions**: Use A² + B² = C² to find the length of one side of the right triangle. Find side AB by using triangle BOA, then find side BC.

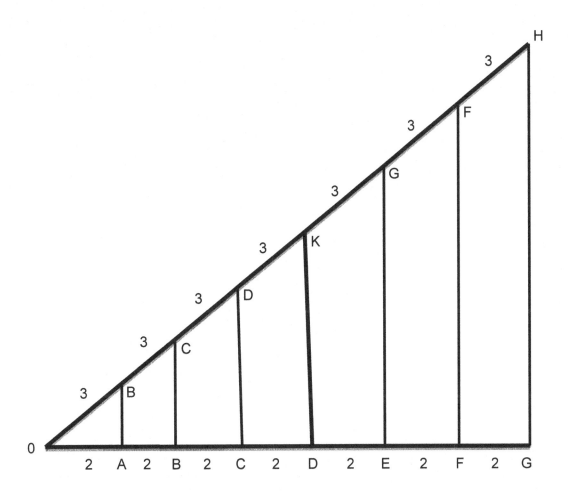

Find sides   1. AB _____ 2. BC _____ 3. CD _____ 4. DE _____

5. DK _____ 6. EG _____ 7. FF _____ 8. GH _____

# Chapter 7

## Polynomials

# Polynomials 1

**Name** _____     **Date** _____

**Directions** Select any two polynomials and add or subtract them. Place letters of the given polynomials on a line below the double lines.

| **A** | **B** | **C** |
|---|---|---|
| $X^2-2X+6$ | $X^2-6X-7$ | $X^3-2X^2+X+1$ |

_____

_____

**1.)** $2X^2-8X-1$    **2.)** $X^3-X^2-X+7$    **3.)** $X^3-X^2-5X-6$    **4.)** $X^3-3X^2+3X-5$    **5.)** $-X^3+3X^2-3X+5$

     +               +              +              -              -

_____

**6.)** $-X^3+3X^2-7X-8$    **7.)** $X^3-3X^2+7X+8$    **8.)** $-4X-13$    **9.)** 0    **10.)** $4X+13$

     -               -              -                               -

_____

**Use A, B, C, above to solve these problems.**

**11.)** $(A+B)-C$      **12.)** $(B+C)-B$      **13.)** $(C+A)-C$      **14.)** $(C+A)-B$

# Polynomials 2

Name _____     Date _____

**Directions**: Find the missing polynomials in the given problems.

$$X^3 + X^2 -2X + 6$$

**1.)** - (_____)

$$2X^2 -4X + 8$$

**2.)** - (_____)

$$X^2 - 7X + 11$$

**3.)** - (_____)

$$-3X^3 + X^2 -9X +14$$

**4.)** - (_____)

$$X^3 +2X^2 - 12X$$

**5.)** - (_____)

$$-X^2 + 6X + 7$$

**6.)** - (_____)

$$3X^2 +3x + 6$$

**7.)** - (_____)

---

$$X^2 + 7x + 11$$

# Polynomials 3

**Name** _____   **Date** _____

**Directions**: Find the sum of each monomial, binomial, trinomial, and others.

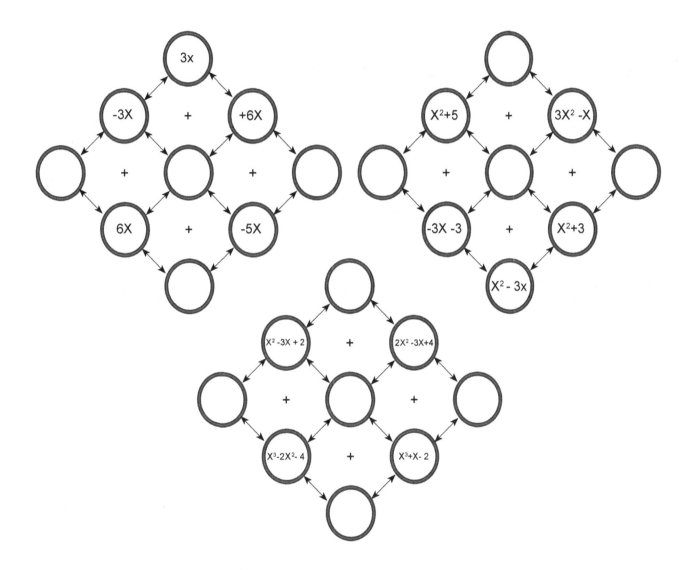

# Polynomials 4

Name _____     Date _____

**Directions**: Arrange the monomials, binomials and trinomials in three groups. Find the sum of each group.

$X^3+X^2-2X+6$          $X^3$               $X^3 + 4$               $X^3 - 4X - 7$

$X^3 + 3X^2+ -6$         $3X^3 - 3X$          $4X^5$                 $X^2 + 3X + 3$

$X^2 -2X- 4$            $-5x^2 - 2X + 2$      $X^2 - 5$              $X^3$

$X^2$                  $X^6 - 6$            $X^4 + 1$              $X^9 - X + 7$

$X^3 - 3$              $X$                  $X^3 -3X + 5$          $X^5 -5X + 4$

$2X^3-25X +19$          $-4X^4 - 5$          $X^2$                  $X^4 + 3X - 6X^3$


**Monomials**                    **Binomials**                    **Trinomials**


_____          _____          _____

146

# Polynomials 5

**Name** _____ **Date** _____

**Directions**: Add or subtract these polynomials in the boxes.

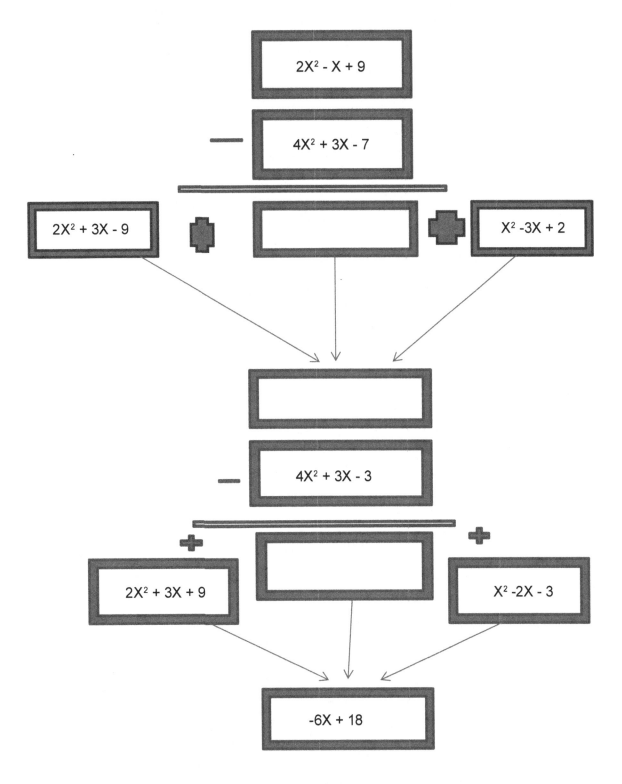

# Chapter 8

Graphing a Coordinate Plane

# Ordered Pairs 1

Name _____    Date _____

**Directions**: Find the ordered pairs and place the points below. Use whole numbers

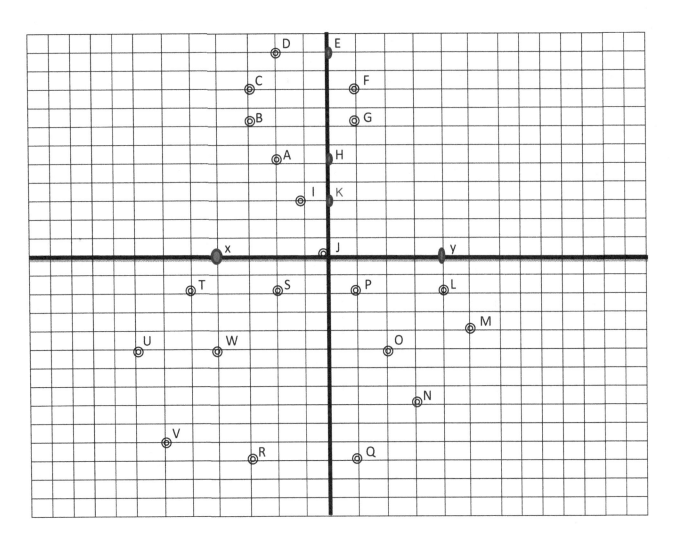

A. (  ,  )    K. (  ,  )    X. (  ,  )

B. (  ,  )    L. (  ,  )    Y. (  ,  )

C. (  ,  )    M. (  ,  )

D. (  ,  )    N. (  ,  )

E. (  ,  )    O. (  ,  )

Y. (  ,  )    P. (  ,  )

G. (  ,  )    Q. (  ,  )

R. (  ,  )    T. (  ,  )

# Ordered Pairs 2

Name _____     Date _____

**Directions**: Find the ordered pairs and graph the points on the X and Y axes.

**A.** (6 − 3, 4 − 4)

**B.** (2 − 1, 4 -5)

**C.** (5 -5, 3x1)

**D.** (-5/5, 6/6)

**E.** (-3(2) +3),7.6

**F.** (8/-4 + 1, -8 /2 + 3)

**G.** (0/10,-3)

**H.** (10 x1 /10, -8/8)

**I.** (6 − 3, 5 - 5)

**J.** (3x3, 6 − 6)

**K.** (3.4 + 6, 8.9 − 4.9)

**L.** (3.3 − 3.3, 8 −(4)

**M.** (-3 ½, 2(1 + 1)

**N.** (-18/2, 6-6)

**O.** (-5 ½ + 2 ½, -8 + 4)

**P.** (3 1/3 - 3 1/3, 6)

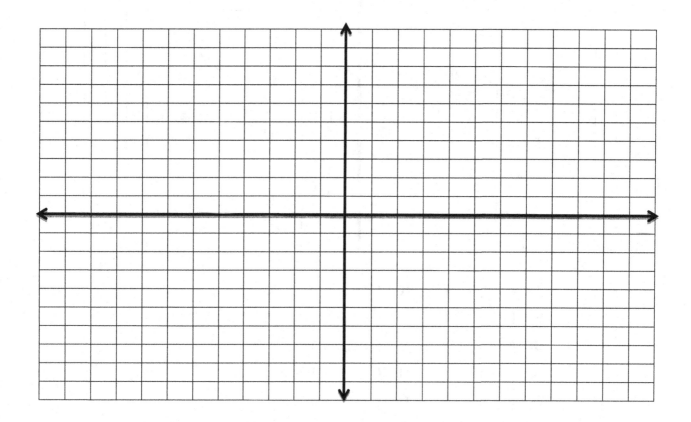

# Ordered Pairs 3

Name _____     Date _____

**Directions**: Locate these points and connect them to form a picture.

**1.** (11 , 0)     **2.** (11 , 3)     **3.** (11 , 4)     **4.** (11 , 5)     **5.** (8 , 4.5)     **6.** (5 , 4.33)     **7.** (3 , 4.33)

**8.** (1 , 4.33)     **9.** (0 , 4.33)     **10.** (-2 , 4.33)     **11.** (-4 , 4.33)     **12.** (-5 , 4.33)     **13.** (-7 , 4)     **14.** (-6 , 5)

**15.** (-5 , 5.8)     **16.** (-4 , 6)     **17.** (-3 , 5)     **18.** (-3 , 6.5)     **19.** (-4 , 8)     **20.** (-6 , 8)     **21.** (-8 , 8)

**22.** (-9 , 6.5)     **23.** (-10 , 4)     **24.** (-11 , 4)     **25.** (-11 , 5.2)     **26.** (-11 , -2)     **27.** (-10 , -2)     **28.** (-9 , -3)

**29.** (-7 , -3)     **30.** (-6 , -3)     **31.** (-5 , -2)     **32.** (-6 , -2)     **33.** (-5 , 0)     **34.** (-2 , 0)     **35.** (0 , 0)

**36.** (2 , -1)     **37.** (4 , -1.5)     **38.** (6 , -1.5)     **39.** (8 , -1)     **40.** (9 , -1)     **41.** (11 , 0)

# Ordered Pairs 4

Name _____     Date _____

**Directions**: Find the ordered pairs for X and Y by solving the equations. Graph these points.

**Point A**   (X + 6 = 8, Y -2 = -8)       **Point E**   (2X +4= 8, -2Y +7 =8)

**Point B**   (-X + 6=8,Y-1.5 = -8)       **Point F**   (-2/3X=7, 2/3Y= -3)

**Point C**   (2X = 12 , 1/2Y = 3)        **Point G**   -2(X-1) = 3(X + 2) , 1/2Y + 3 = 2(Y + 3)

**Point D**   (4X = 36,-2Y=12)            **Point H**   (-2/4 X – 2 = 1 , -1/2Y + 2 = -1)

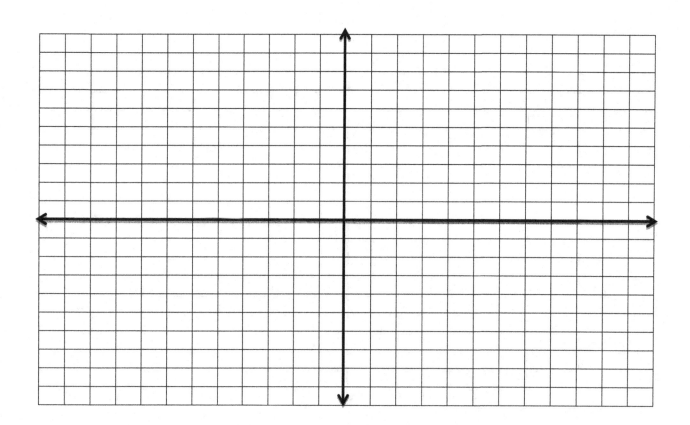

# Distance Formula 1

**Name** _____     **Date** _____

**Directions**: Find the distance around the city from A to K and K to A.

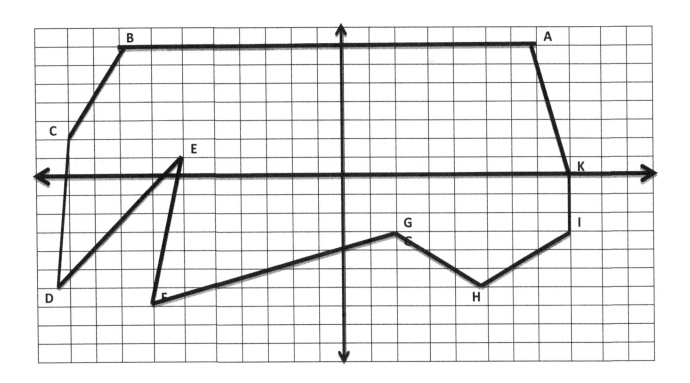

1. AB _____     2. BC _____     3. CD _____     4. DE _____     5. EF _____

6. FG _____     7. GH _____     8. HI _____     9. IK _____     10. KA _____

# Distance Formula 2

**Name** _____  **Date** _____

**Directions**: Find the perimeter of the figure by using the distance formula.

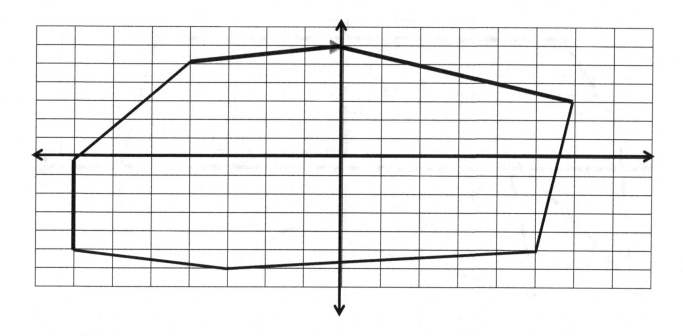

**The perimeter is** _____

# Slopes of Lines 1

**Name** _____    **Date** _____

**Directions**: Find the slope of each line.

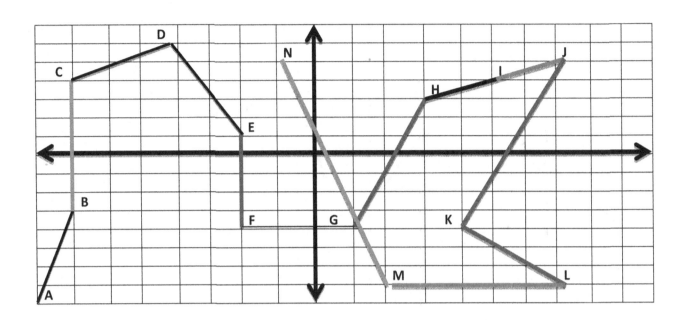

1. AB _____    2. BC _____    3. CD _____    4. DE _____    5. EF _____

6. FG _____    7. GH _____    8. HJ _____    9. JK _____    10. LM _____

11. MN _____

# Slopes of Lines 2

Name _____    Date _____

**Directions**: Find the slopes in each quadrant. Write the slope beside the line.

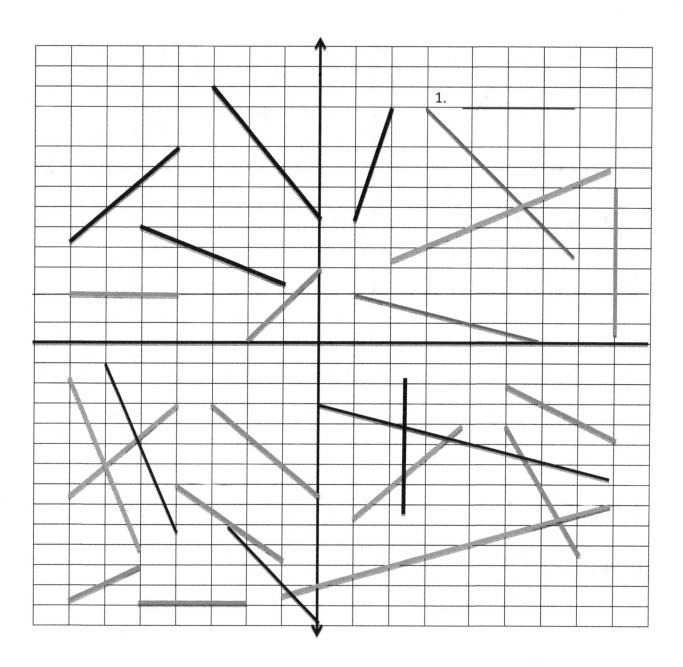

Find the slopes of the lines.

1.    2.    3.    4.    5.    6.    7.    8.    9.    10.    11.    12.    13.    14.

15.    16.    17.    18.    19.    20.    21.    22.    23.    24.    25.

# Slopes of Lines 3

Name _____     Date _____

**Directions**: Find the slope of each line. Use a line to connect two pairs.

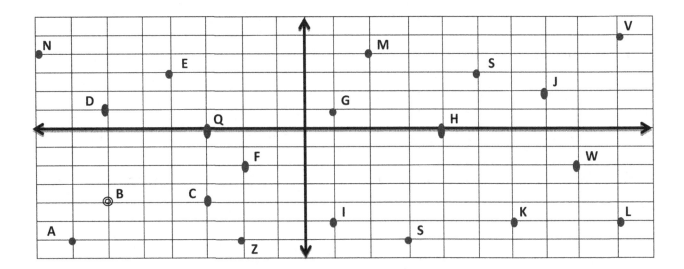

1. <u>AB = 2/1</u>     2. _____     3. _____     4. _____     5. _____     6. _____     7. _____

8. _____     9. _____     10. _____     11. _____     12. _____     13. _____     14. _____

15. _____     16. _____     17. _____     18. _____

# Slopes of Lines 4

Name _____    Date _____

**Directions**: Find the slope. Place each letter in the correct answer box.

| **Red** | **Red** | **Yellow** | **Yellow** |
|---|---|---|---|
| **A.** (4 , 3); (9 , 4) | **B.** (3 , 1); (9 , - 2) | **C.** (1 , 0) ; (2 , 2) | **D.** (- 4 , 2) ; (3 , -2) |

| **Blue** | **Blue** | **Green** | **Green** |
|---|---|---|---|
| **E.** (3 , 2); (7 , 1) | **F.** (3 , 2); (-5 , 1) | **G.** (1 , 1); (2 , 1) | **H.** (3 , 2) ; (4 , 3) |

| **Orange** | **Orange** | **Brown** | **Brown** |
|---|---|---|---|
| **I.** (4 , 8) ; (4 , 5) | **J.** (3 , -2) ;(-1 , 5) | **K.** (-4 , 1) ; (-3 , 7) | **L.** (7 , -4) ;(8 , 0) |

| **Black** | **Black** | **Red** | **Green** |
|---|---|---|---|
| **M.** (6 , 5) ; (4 , 5) | **N.** (-4 , 1) ; (5 , 7) | **O.** (3 , 2) ; (6 , 1) | **P.** (3 ,5); (-5 , -3) |

| .20 | -.59 | -.50 | 5 | 4 | 2 | 1.75 | 3 | .75 |
|---|---|---|---|---|---|---|---|---|
| -.25 | 0 | 1 | NA | 0 | 8 | 6 | -1.75 | -2 |
| -.33 | -1 | -.57 | -6 | -7 | .125 | .67 | 1 | 0 |

# Slopes of Lines 5

**Name** _____     **Date** _____

**Directions**: Find the slopes using the given equations for the clocks.

1.  Y = -3X +2
2.  Y = 6X - 4
3.  X - Y = 8
4.  X + Y = -7
5.  1/4X + 3/6 Y = 9
6.  3X - 3/6 Y = -8

```
        11  12   1                   -11 -12   0
      10            2              -10            -1
      9       0       3            -9       0    -2
      8               5            -8            -3
          7  0  Ø  6                   Ø -7 -6 -5
```

7.  2X + 3Y = 6
8.  -2X + 3Y = -3
9.  X = 5
10. Y = -3
11. 3/5X + 1/3Y = 2

```
        11   0   12                  -11   0  -12
      10    Ø       1              -10            -1
      9       0       2            - 9       0      - 2
      8               3            -8             - 3
          7  6  5  4                  - 7 -6  - 5 -4
```

12. 2/3X - 4/5Y = 6
13. 2X + 3/4Y = -5
14. X + 4/5 Y = 4
15. 2/6 X - Y = 6

```
              ± 11      ± 12
        ± 10                ±1
      ± 9          0          ± 2
      ± 8                    ± 3
        ± 7                ± 4
          0    ± 6   ± 5
```

161

# Slopes and y-intercepts 6

**Name** _____ **Date** _____

**Directions**: Use the equations to find the slope and y-intercept. Place the equations , slope and the y-Intercept in the boxes below.

| 1. Orange | 2. Green | 3. Blue | 4. Yellow |
|---|---|---|---|
| $Y = 2X + 3$ | $Y = 3/4X - 1$ | $2X + Y = 7$ | $2Y = 6X - 8$ |

| 5. Purple | 6. Tan | 7. Brown | 8. Red |
|---|---|---|---|
| $X = 2$ | $Y = 6$ | $1/2X + 1/3Y = 1$ | $X + 1/3Y = 6$ |

$M = 2$   $M = 3/4$   $M = 3$   $M = 6$   $M = o$   $M = -3/2$   $M = -2$

$B = -4$   $M = ¼$   $B = 3$   $B = 16$   $B = 0$   $B = .3$   $B = 18$

$B = 7$   $M = -3$   $B = 6$   $M = ¾$   $B = -6$

| Orange | Green | Blue | Yellow | Purple | Tan | Brown | Red |
|---|---|---|---|---|---|---|---|
|  |  |  |  |  |  |  |  |
|  |  |  |  |  |  |  |  |
|  |  |  |  |  |  |  |  |
|  |  |  |  |  |  |  |  |

# Equations of Lines 7

**Name** _____     **Date** _____

**Directions**: Match the equations and graphs by placing the letter beside the equations below.

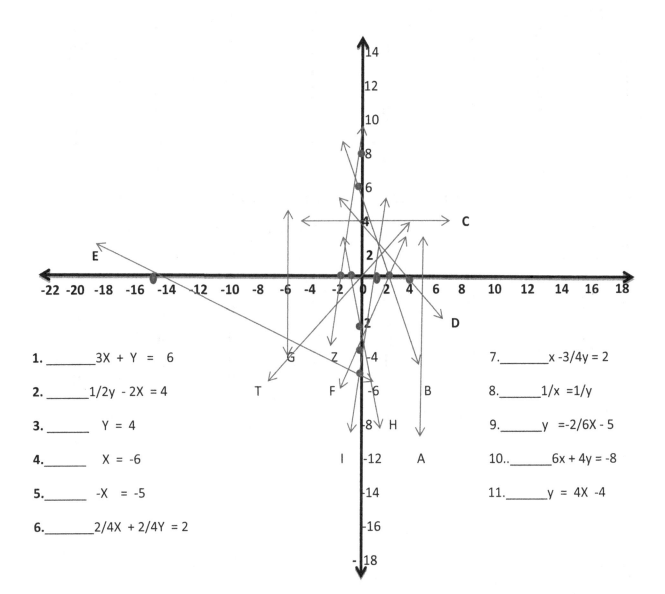

1. _____$3X + Y = 6$

2. _____$1/2y - 2X = 4$

3. _____ $Y = 4$

4. _____ $X = -6$

5. _____ $-X = -5$

6. _____$2/4X + 2/4Y = 2$

7. _____$x - 3/4y = 2$

8. _____$1/x = 1/y$

9. _____$y = -2/6X - 5$

10.. _____$6x + 4y = -8$

11. _____$y = 4X - 4$

# Equations of Lines 8

**Name** _____     **Date** _____

**Directions**: Graph these points to make a kite. Then use problems 5, 6, 7, and 8, to form four triangles.
Color the triangles.

1.

| X | Y |
|---|---|
| 0 | 6 |
| 4 | 0 |

2.

| X | Y |
|---|---|
| 0 | 6 |
| -4 | 0 |

3.

| X | Y |
|---|---|
| -4 | 0 |
| 0 | -6 |

4.

| X | Y |
|---|---|
| 4 | 0 |
| 0 | -6 |

5.

| X | Y |
|---|---|
| 0 | 3 |
| -5 | 3 |

6.

| X | Y |
|---|---|
| 0 | -3 |
| 2 | -3 |

7.

| X | Y |
|---|---|
| -2 | 0 |
| -2 | -3 |

8.

| X | Y |
|---|---|
| 2 | 0 |
| 2 | -4 |

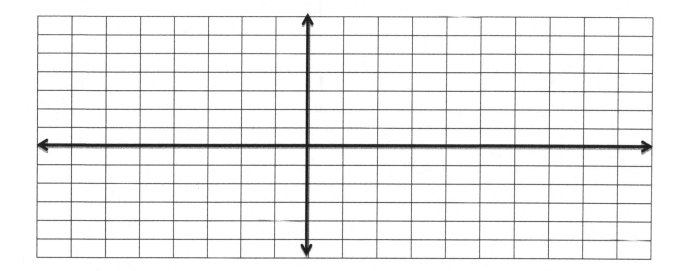

# Equations of Lines 9

Name _____    Date _____

**Directions**: Graph these equations by using the X and Y intercepts. Find all equations that will touch the box.

**1.** $X + Y = 2$    **2.** $2X + 3Y = 6$    **3.** $1/2X + 1/3Y = -1$    **4.** $2X - Y = 6$    **5.** $2x - 3Y = 6$

**6.** $1/2X - 3Y = 2$    **7.** $\frac{1}{2}(X - 4) = Y + 2$    **8.** $X - Y = 4$    **9.** $6X + 2Y = 8$    **10.** $8X - 4Y = 18$

**11.** $X/5 = 4/5$    **12.** $X = 4Y$    **13.** $4X - 3Y = 12$    **14.** $Y = 4X$    **15.** $1/6X = 1.2$

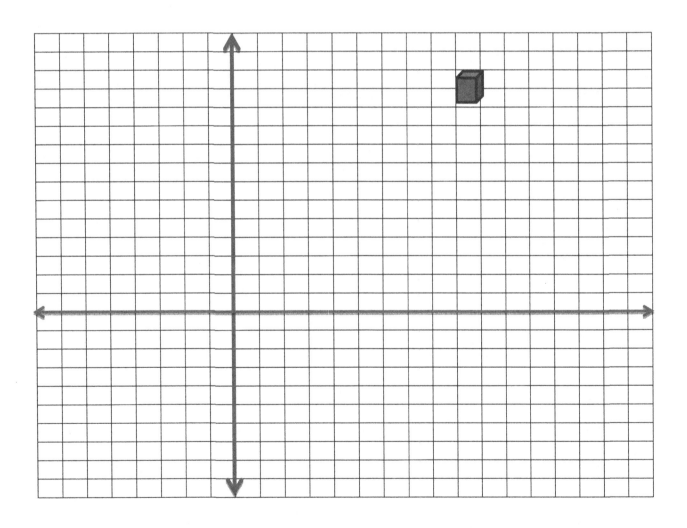

# Equations of Lines 10

**Directions**: Find the X and Y intercept for each equation. Write the letter for the correct X and Y intercept.

**(A)**

$3X + 2Y = -6$

**(B)**

$1/2X + 1/3Y = 2$

**(C)**

$1/2X - Y = 6$

**(D)**

$X = 4$

**(E)**

$Y = 4$

**(F)**

$X + 2/3Y = -4$

**(G)**

$5X - 6Y = 10$

**(H)**

$3/4X - 3Y = 12$

**(I)**

$-4X - 5Y = 20$

**(J)**

$.3X - 6Y = 6$

| | | | | |
|---|---|---|---|---|
| _____ | _____ | _____ | _____ | _____ |
| 0    -3 | 0    -4 | 0    -1 | 0    6 | 0    -1 2/3 |
| -2    0 | -5    0 | 20    0 | 4    0 | 2    0 |

| | | | | |
|---|---|---|---|---|
| _____ | _____ | _____ | _____ | _____ |
| 0    -6 | 0    -6 | 0    4 | 4    0 | 0    -4 |
| 12    0 | -4    0 | -1    4 | 4    -2 | 16    0 |

## Equations of Lines 11

**Name** _____   **Date** _____

**Directions**: Graph these equations. Place the answers on the given axis.

**1.** $Y = X$

**2.** $Y = -6$

**3.** $Y = 2X$

**4.** $X = 4$

**5.** $1 / 3\, X = -4$

**6.** $Y = 2 /3\, X$

**7.** $X + Y = 8$

**8.** $2X - 4Y = 12$

**9.** $X + 2 / 5\, Y = 5$

**10.** $X / 3 + Y / 4 = 3$

**11.** $2(X + 3) -3y = -6$

**1.**      **2.**      **3.**      **4.**      **5.**

**6.**      **7.**      **8.**      **9.**      **10.**      **11.**

# Linear Equations 1

Name _____     Date _____

**Directions**: Use the color green to identify all linear equations.

| | | | |
|---|---|---|---|
| $X + Y = 6$ | $Y = 8 - X$ | $2X - Y = 6$ | $X + Y/2 = 7$ |
| $X + Y = -4$ | $Y = -2/3\ X + 3$ | $1/3X + 2/3\ Y = 3$ | $X = -8$ |
| $1/XY = 17$ | $Y = 1/3X$ | $Y = X$ | $Y = 0$ |
| $Y = X - 1$ | $Y = -X$ | $Y = 2$ | $(X + Y)/Y$ |
| $XY = 4$ | $X/Y = Y/X$ | $2X + 3Y = Y$ | $2/3(X - 5) = 9$ |
| $Y = X^2$ | $X = y^2$ | $X - x/y = 2$ | $Y = |X + 3|$ |
| $2y^2 = X^2$ | $Y = 1/2X^2 + 7$ | $Y = -2x + \sqrt{2}$ | $X - Y = .8$ |

# Linear Equations 2

**Name** _____    **Date** _____

**Directions**: Graph these equations using the X and Y intercepts. Find the box, kite, and octagon.

**A.** X = 3, X = -3, Y = 3 , Y = -3    **B.** 3X + 2Y =12 , 3X − 2Y = -12, 3X − 2Y = 12 ,3X +2Y=-12

**C.** X + y =6 , x + y = -6 , x − y = -6, x − y = 6

    X = 4 , X = -4 ,Y = 4 , Y = -4

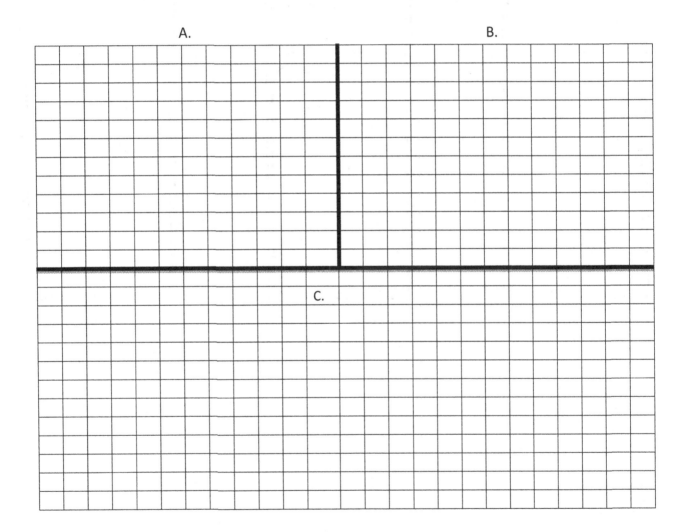

# Equations and Graphs 1

**Name** _____ **Date** _____

**Directions**: Find the slope, y-intercept, X-intercept, and standard form. Create a table and graph them.

1.

| Points | |
|---|---|
| (0 , 3) | (4 , 0) |

| Slope | Equation |
|---|---|

| X and Y - intercepts |
|---|

| Table | Graph |
|---|---|

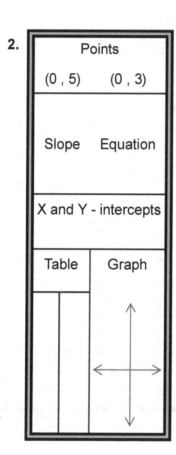

2.

| Points | |
|---|---|
| (0 , 5) | (0 , 3) |

| Slope | Equation |
|---|---|

| X and Y - intercepts |
|---|

| Table | Graph |
|---|---|

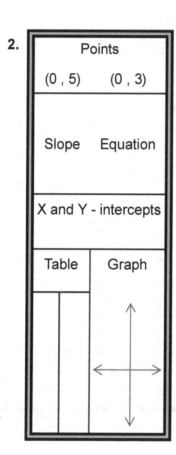

3.

| Points | |
|---|---|
| (5 , 0) | (3 , 0) |

| Slope | Equation |
|---|---|

| X and Y - intercepts |
|---|

| Table | Graph |
|---|---|

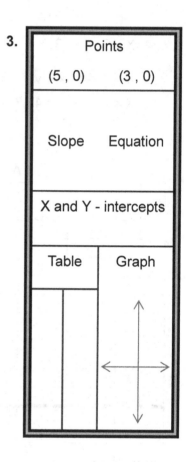

# Equations and Graphs 2

**Name** _____  **Date** _____

**Directions**: Find the slope, y-intercept, X-intercept, and standard form. Create a table and graph them.

**1.**

| Points | |
|---|---|
| (2 , 3) | (4 , 2) |

| Slope | Equation |
|---|---|
|  |  |

| X and Y - intercepts | |
|---|---|

| Table | Graph |
|---|---|
|  |  |

**2.**

| Points | |
|---|---|
| (6 , 7) | (4 , 9) |

| Slope | Equation |
|---|---|
|  |  |

| X and Y - intercepts | |
|---|---|

| Table | Graph |
|---|---|
|  |  |

**3.**

| Points | |
|---|---|
| (2/3 , 3) | (2/4 , -2/3) |

| Slope | Equation |
|---|---|
|  |  |

| X and Y - intercepts | |
|---|---|

| Table | Graph |
|---|---|
|  |  |

# Zeros of the Functions 1

Name _____  Date _____

**Directions**: Using the designated colors, find the zeros of the functions and their answers in the picture.

**1.** F(x) = 2X -3   Green

**2.** F(x) = 3X + 3   Gray

**3.** F(x) = 5X + 1   Blue

**4.** F(x) = 10X   Yellow

**5.** F(x) = -2/3 X - 7   Orange

**6.** F(x) = 1/X - 2   Red

**7.** F(x) = X - 1   Brown

**8.** F(x) = 3(5 - X )   Black

**9.** F(x) = 3(X-5)   Red

**10.** F(x) = 2X + 6   Pink

**11.** F(x) = 1/2X + 6   Purple

**12.** F(X) = 6   White

**13.** F(x) = 2X - 5X - 7   Tan

**14.** F(x) = ( X - 1)( X + 2 )   Pink

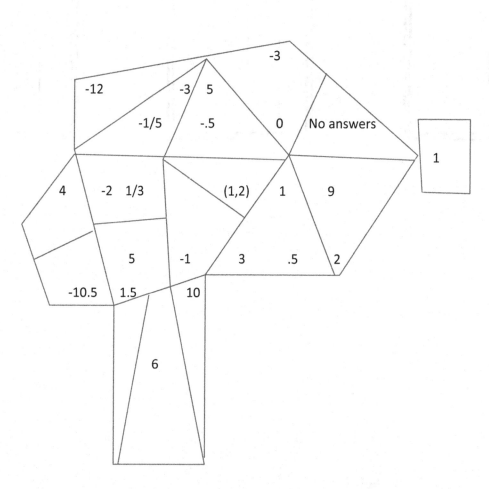

172

# Chapter 9

# Systems of Linear Equations

# System of Equations 1

**Name** _____  **Date** _____

**Directions**: First find the slopes and Y-intercepts for A – J. Then you must indicate whether the equations are crossing, following, perpendicular, or parallel to each other by placing a X or check mark. Next, indicate whether the equations are consistent/independent, inconsistent or consistent/dependent for the systems of equations by placing the correct answer in the terminology column.

**A.**  X + 2Y = -10  **B.**  X = 2  **C.**  3X + y = 4  **D.**  Y = 2  **E.**  1/2X + Y = -5

**F.**  2X + 4Y = 6  **G.**  3Y- X = -6  **H.**  2/4X + Y = 5  **I.**  3X -Y = -1  **J.**  X = - 3

| Equations: | A | B | C | D | E | F | G | H | I | J |
|---|---|---|---|---|---|---|---|---|---|---|
| Slopes: | ___ | ___ | ___ | ___ | ___ | ___ | ___ | ___ | ___ | ___ |
| Y-intercepts: | ___ | ___ | ___ | ___ | ___ | ___ | ___ | ___ | ___ | ___ |

| Equations | Crossing | Parallel | Following | Perpendicular | Terminology |
|---|---|---|---|---|---|
| C  and  G | _____ | _____ | _____ | _____ | _____ |
| A  and  J | _____ | _____ | _____ | _____ | _____ |
| E  and  I | _____ | _____ | _____ | _____ | _____ |
| A  and  C | _____ | _____ | _____ | _____ | _____ |
| A  and  F | _____ | _____ | _____ | _____ | _____ |
| A  and  I | _____ | _____ | _____ | _____ | _____ |
| B  and  J | _____ | _____ | _____ | _____ | _____ |
| E  and  F | _____ | _____ | _____ | _____ | _____ |
| A  and  H | _____ | _____ | _____ | _____ | _____ |
| F  and  I | _____ | _____ | _____ | _____ | _____ |
| A  and  E | _____ | _____ | _____ | _____ | _____ |
| F  and  H | _____ | _____ | _____ | _____ | _____ |
| B  and  J | _____ | _____ | _____ | _____ | _____ |

# Systems of Equations 2

**Directions**: Select any two equations and solve for X and Y. Solve these equations by the substitution method.

**A.** $1/2X + 3Y = 6$        **B.** $X + 2Y = 2$        **C.** $X + 2/3Y = -4$        **D.** $2/2X + 1/3 Y = -7$

**E.** $X - Y = 4$        **F.** $X + 1/4Y = 6$        **G.** $1/2X - 3Y = 8$        **H.** $1/4X - 1/3 Y = -2$

**I.** $y = 1/2x + 3$        **J.** $x = 1/4$        **K.** $y = -4$

1. Do   A   and   B

2. Do   E   and   B

3. Do   D   and   H

4. Do   F   and   G

5. Do   E   and   G

6. Do   A   and   H

7. Do   C   and   F

8. Do   D   and   J

9. Do   B   and   E

# Solving Equations for X and Y 3

Name _____     Date _____

**Directions**: Solve the equations for X and Y. Place the answers in the boxes below. Use any method to find X and y.

| 1. | 2. | 3. | 4. |
|---|---|---|---|
| $2X + 3Y = 6$ | $X + 1/2X - Y = 4$ | $X = 6$ | $X + 3Y = 6$ |
| $X - 3Y = 6$ | $1/2X - Y = 6$ | $Y = -1$ | $2X - Y = 4$ |

| 5. | 6. | 7. | 8. |
|---|---|---|---|
| $3X + Y = 2/3$ | $X + Y = 4$ | $Y = 2X - 3$ | $x = 2$ |
| $X + 2Y = 2$ | $X - Y = 4$ | $X - Y = 3$ | $X = 3$ |

| 9. | 10. | 11. |
|---|---|---|
| $Y = 2X - 3$ | $1/2X + 1/3Y = 2$ | $-2X + 4Y = 12$ |
| $X + 2/4Y = 2$ | $X + 1/3 Y = 2$ | $Y = 3X$ |

|       | 1. | 2. | 3. | 4. | 5. | 6. | 7 | 8. | 9. | 10. | 11. |
|-------|----|----|----|----|----|----|---|----|----|-----|-----|
| X =   |    |    |    |    |    |    |   |    |    |     |     |
| Y =   |    |    |    |    |    |    |   |    |    |     |     |

# Systems of Equations 4

**Name** _____     **Date** _____

**Directions**: Select any two equations and solve for X and Y. Graph the equations. Use your own paper.

**1.** 1/2X + 3Y = 5      **2.** X - 2Y = 2      **3.** X + 2Y = - 4      **4.** 2X + Y = -7

**5.** 3X + Y = 4      **6.** 3X + 2Y = 6      **7.** 2/3X - 1/3Y = 2      **8.** 5X + Y = -2

**A.**
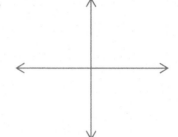

**B.**
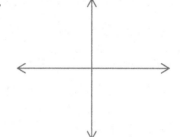

**C.**
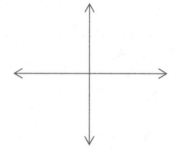

**D.**
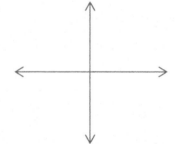

**E.**
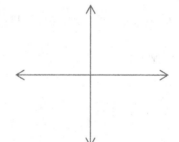

**F.**
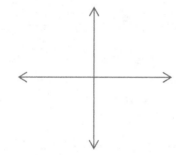

**G.**
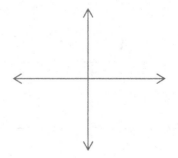

**H.**
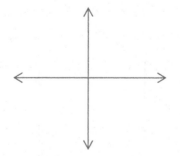

**I.**
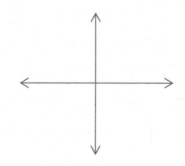

# Function or Not a Function 1

Name _____    Date _____

**Directions**: Use a colored pencil to identify the functions. Write Yes if it is a function. Write No if it is not a function. Place the answers in the boxes.

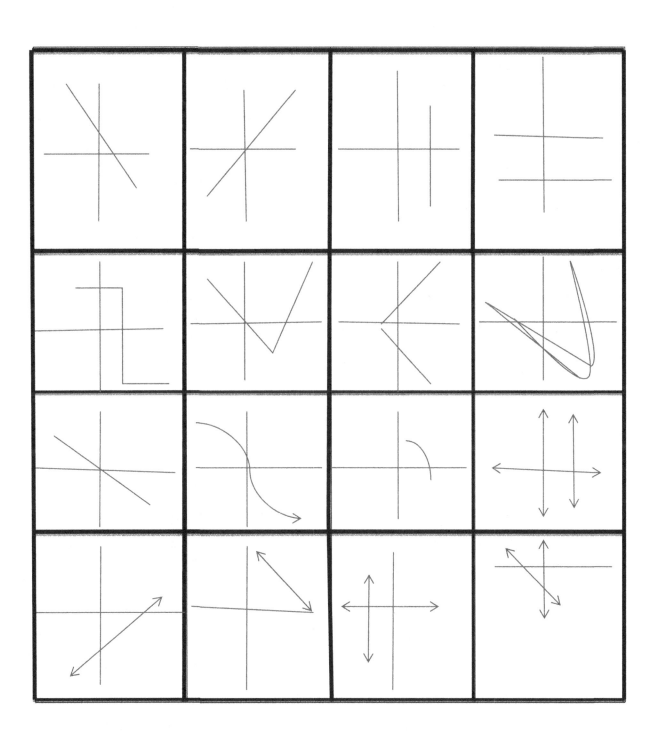

# Function or Not a Function

**Name** _____    **Date** _____

**Directions**: Use any color to identify the functions. Write Yes if it is a function. Write No if it is not a function. Place the answers in the boxes.

| X = 8 | Y = -7 | X + 2Y = 4 | X - 2Y = 4 | 2/3X + 3Y =3 |
|---|---|---|---|---|
| X \| Y | X \| Y | X \| Y | | |
| 2 \| 4 <br> 3 \| 6 <br> 4 \| 8 | 6 \| 0 <br> 6 \| -4 <br> 6 \| 1/4 | 8 \| 9 <br> 7 \| 6 <br> -7 \| 5 | | |
| | | | | |
| | | | | |

# Chapter 10

## Variations

# Variations

**Name** _____    **Date** _____

**Directions**: Solve these variations and place the answers on the given lines.

### Direct Variations

$$Y = K x$$

1. If y is 12 when x is 2, find y when x is 2.
2. If y is -6 when x is -3, find y when x is 6.
3. If y is 2 when x is 20, find y when x is 30.
4. If y is 3 when x is 30, find y when x is 4.

Direct Variations

1. _____ 2. _____ 3. _____ 4. _____

### Inverse Variations

$$Y = K/x$$

1. If y is 20 when x is 4, find y when x is 4.
2. If y is 30 when x is 1, find y when x is 4.
3. If y is -8 when x is 5, find y when x is 6.
4. If y is 40 when x is 15, find y when x is 6.

Inverse Variations

1. _____ 2. _____ 3. _____ 4. _____

### Direct and Inverse Variations as the Square of x

$$Y = Kuv/s^2$$

1. If y is 20 when u is 3, v is 5 and s is 2,
   find y when u is 3, v is 2 and s is 3,

2. If y is 8 when u is 3, v is 2 and s is 2,
   find y when u is 2, v is 4 and s is 4,

Direct and Inverse Variations as the Square of x

1. _____ 2. _____

$$Y = K x^2$$

1. If y is 40 when x is 2,
   find y when x is 2.

2. If y is 30 when x is 3,
   find y when x is ½.

Direct as the square of X

1. _____ 2. _____

# Chapter 11

## Matrices

# Matrices 1

**Name** _____   **Date** _____

**Directions**: Find the sums , differences , and scalar numbers for these matrices.

Put matrices at the top a-f

**A.** $\begin{pmatrix} 1 & 3 \\ 5 & 7 \end{pmatrix}$  **B.** $\begin{pmatrix} 2 & 3 \\ 5 & 7 \end{pmatrix}$  **C.** $\begin{pmatrix} -1 & -2 \\ -3 & -4 \end{pmatrix}$  **D.** $\begin{pmatrix} -1 & 4 \\ -5 & -2 \end{pmatrix}$  **E.** $\begin{pmatrix} 1 & 0 \\ 0 & 1 \end{pmatrix}$  **F.** $\begin{pmatrix} 8 & -6 \\ -7 & -5 \end{pmatrix}$

**1.** Find   A + B

**2.** Find   B + C

**3.** Find   C - D

**4.**   Find   A - B

**5.** Find   E + C

**6.** Find   A + C

**7.** Find   2A - 3C

**8.**   Find   1 /2 A

**9.** Find   - 1 / 2 A

**10.** Find   4B - 4C

**11.** Find   -5 B + 3 F

**12.** Find   -2/3 D

**13.** Find   1 /2 (A + D - C)

**14.** Find   .6 B - .3 C

**15.** Find   3A - 2 C

**16.** Find   2 E + .4 B

187

# Matrices 2

Name _____     Date _____

**Directions**: Write the number of each problem in the appropriate block.

1. $R_2C_4$

2. $R_2C_5$

3. $R_3C_6$

4. $R_8C_4$

5. $R_4C_3$

6. $R_8C_7$

7. $R_2C_6$

8. $R_6C_1$

9. $R_5C_3$

10. $R_7C_7$

11. $R_2C_7$

12. $R_6C_3$

13. $R_6C_2$

14. $R_5C_7$

15. $R_8C_3$

16. $R_8C_3$

17. $R_3C_7$

18. $R_4C_3$

19. $R_1C_8$

20. $R_1C_8$

21. $R_8C_8$

22. $R_8C_8$

23. $R_2C_2$

24. $R_4C_4$

25. $R_3C_8$

26. $R_3C_5$

27. $R_6C_6$

28. $R_8C_1$

29. $R_2C_1$

30. $R_7C_6$

31. $R_3C_1$

32. $R_4C_1$

33. $R_5C_1$

34. $R_7C_5$

35. RC

36. $R_8C_2$

37. $R_8C_5$

38. $R_6C_5$

39. $R_1C_8$

40. $R_4C_5$

|  |  |  |  |  |  |  |  |
|--|--|--|--|--|--|--|--|
|  |  |  |  |  |  |  |  |
|  |  |  |  |  |  |  |  |
|  |  |  |  |  |  |  |  |
|  |  |  |  |  |  |  |  |
|  |  |  |  |  |  |  |  |
|  |  |  |  |  |  |  |  |
|  |  |  |  |  |  |  |  |
|  |  |  |  |  |  |  |  |

# Matrices 3

**Name** _____     **Date** _____

**Directions**: Identify these words at the given locations by using rows and columns.

| | | | |
|---|---|---|---|
| Car | Girl'sFace | Box | Hat |
| Ball | Truck | Kite | Eight |
| Ring | Ring | Boat | Pin |
| Bike | Shoes | Boy | Comb |

**1.** $R_2C_1$ _____

**2.** $R_4C_2$ _____

**3.** $R_1C_3$ _____

**4.** $R_1C_3$ _____

**5.** $R_3C_2$ _____

**6.** $R_4C_1$ _____

**7.** $R_1C_1$ _____

**8.** $R_2C_2$ _____

**9.** $R_3C_1$ _____

**9a.** $R_1C_4$ _____

**10.** $R_1C_2$ _____

**11.** $R_2C_3$ _____

**12.** $R_3C_3$ _____

**13.** $R_3C_4$ _____

**14.** $R_4C_4$ _____

**15.** $R_2C_1$ _____

**16.** $R_4C_4$ _____

**17.** $R_4C_3$ _____

**18.** $R_3C_2$ _____

**19.** $R_1C_2$ _____

**20.** $R_4C_3$ _____

**21.** $R_3C_4$ _____

**22.** $RC_2$ _____

**23.** $R_2C_4$ _____

**24.** $R_4C_1$ _____

**25.** $R_3C_3$ _____

**26.** $R_3C_2$ _____

189

# Chapter 12

## Mode, Median and Average

# Mode

**Name** _____   **Date** _____

**Directions**: Find the mode by using these letters. Write the letters on the given lines. What is the message?

1. A, M, M, M, M, H, U, Y, E, T, M, T, T, and X     ____M____

2. C, F, T, D, Y, A, C, W, A, H, A, T, A, and S     ____A____

3. C, U, R, C, O, O, T, R, E, T, D, T, and F     ____T____

4. C, T, U, H, H, I, R, H, H, X, T, U, H, H, X, Z, and C     ____H____

5. A, A, E, Y, E, G, Y, U, and E     ____E____

6. A, D, F, U, R, M, T, M, M, O, I, P, M, M, F, and A     ____M____

7. Z, X, V, B, N, H, K, G, A, A, A, J, U, A, A, J, U, A, A, A, and Y     ____A____

8. D, F, T, E, T, Y, T, E, D, T, T, T, and W     ____T____

9. A, R, J, E, Y, I, I, I, R, and I     ____I____

10. Z, S, R, I, P, P, C, D, C, C, C, C, G, and T     ____C____

11. A, G, S, U, T, S, S, P, and F     ____S____

---

12. S, R, Y, U, C, C, C, C, R, T, and X     ____C____

13. S, G, A, Y, A, R, U, and A     ____A____

14 B, U, O, N, N, N, P, R, and E     ____N____

---

15. H, B, B, U, P, P, B, R, and B     ____B____

16. U, T, E, E, Y, E, U, E, S, and W     ____E____

---

17. F, F, F, F, F, M, and F     ____F____

18. U, U, N, A, U, and E     ____U____

19. N, N, y, W, T, and N     ____N____

---

**Message** _____

# Median

**Name** _____     **Date** _____

**Directions**: Find the median in each given set. Then add the three medians.

**1.** ( 27 , 54 , 22 , 17 , 28 , 90 , 52 )     _____

**2.** ( 28 , 53 , 92 , 28 , 94 , 38 , 91 , 93 , 62 )     _____

**3.** ( 1 , 53 , 48 , 87 , 98 , 54 , 2 , 6 )     _____

**_____**

**4.** ( 107 , 111 , 307 , 453 , 32 , 78 , 4 , 8 )     _____

**5.** ( 6 , 43 , 7 , 98 , 65 , 43 , 2 )     _____

**6.** ( 4 , 6 , 98 , 23 , 34 , 5 )     _____

**_____**

**7.** ( 3 , 5 , 6 , 9 , 4 , 7 , 9 , 4 , 1 , 1 , 6 , 8 , 5 )     _____

**8.** ( 1 , 3 , 7 , 8 , 9 , 4 , 8 , 9 , 4 , 1 )     _____

**9.** ( 4 , 6 , 4 , 7 , 3 , 3 , 7 , 3 , 3 , 9 , 5 , 4 , 8 , 6 , 4 , 2 , 5 , 32 )     _____

**_____**

**10.** ( 3 , 5 , 1 , 2 , 4 , 3 , 1 )     _____

**11.** ( 2 , 4 , 1 , 6 , 3 , 2 )     _____

**12.** ( 2 , 5 , 2 , 1 )     _____

**_____**

**13.** ( 1 , 1 , 1 , 1 , 3 , 4 , 2 , 1 6 , 1 , 21 , 10 , and 68 )     _____

**14.** ( 2 , 3 , 4 , 4 , 6 , 7 3 . 2 , 3 , 76 , 3 , 2 , and 2     _____

**_____**

## Averages

**Name** _____   **Date** _____

**Directions**: Find the average in each set. Subtract the two averages. Show your work.

**1.** ( 1 , 30 , 29 , 17 , 16 ) - ( 36 , 35 , 30 , 17 , 15 , 4 )      18.6   -   22.8   =   -4.2

**2.** ( 4 , 2 , 1 , 4 , 6 , 9 , 3 ) – ( 1 , 2 , 4 , 5 , 10 , 17 , 17 , 21 )    _____ - _____ = _____

**3.** ( 2 , 3 , 3 , 8 , 5 , - 5 , - 4 , 2 , -5 , -2 , 6 ) - ( 3 , 6 , 8 )    _____ - _____ = _____

**4.** ( 3 , 4 , 1 , 5 , 8 , 6 , 9 ) – ( 4 , 3 , 6 , 5 , 4 )    _____ - _____ = _____

**5.** ( 81 , 45 , 43 , 564 ) - ( 987 , 453 , 32 , 9 )    _____ - _____ = _____

**6.** ( 5 , 6 , 7 , 9 , 6 ) - ( - 6 , 7 , 4 , 7 , 8 )    _____ - _____ = _____

**7.** ( 3 , 6 , 7 , - 7 , 9 , 10 ) - ( -4 , 6 , - 6 )    _____ - _____ = _____

**8.** ( 8 , 9 , 5 , 7 , 98 ) - ( - 6 , - 8 , 87 , - 98 )    _____ - _____ = _____

**9.** ( - 5 , - 6 , 7 ) - ( 6 , 8 , 4 , - 7 , 5 , 9 )    _____ - _____ = _____

**10.** ( 987 , 765 , 654 , 67 , 1 ) - ( - 76 , 78 )    _____ - _____ = _____

**11.** ( 3 , 6 , 7 , 9 , 5 , - 4 – 5 ) - ( 4 , 6 , 2 , - 6 )    _____ - _____ = _____

**12.** ( 5 , 6 , 7 , 9 , 54 , ) – ( -5 , -6 , -9 )    _____ - _____ = _____

**13.** ( 4 , 6 , 7 , 8 ) - ( 4 , 6 , 79 )    _____ - _____ = _____

**14.** ( 5 , 5 , 5 , 5 , 6 ) – ( 2 , 3 , 4 , 6 , 7 , 3 , 3 , 7 )    _____ - _____ = _____

**15.** ( 54 , 76 ) - ( 100 , 65 )    _____ - _____ = _____

**16.** ( 432 , 65 ) – ( -76 , -54 )    _____ - _____ = _____

**17.** ( 5 5/4 , 5 ¼ ) - ( 3 2/3 , 5 5/4 )    _____ - _____ = _____

**18.** ( -5 ¾ , + 5 3/3 ) - ( 2 2/5 , - 5 2/3 )    _____ - _____ = _____

**19.** ( 6.87 , 5.43 , 2.43 , 8.54 ) - ( .43 , .543 , .87 )    _____ - _____ = _____

**20.** ( 12.76 , 56. 43 , 65.98 ) – ( .76.98 , - 54.78 )    _____ - _____ = _____

**21.** ( 7.54 , .98 , 5.54 ) - ( 43 , 67 , 8.87 )    _____ - _____ = _____

**22.** ( 4 2/5 , -7 4/4 ) - ( - 4 2/4 , 2 4/3 )    _____ - _____ = _____

**23.** ( 1 , 2 , 1 , 1 , 3 , 1 ) - ( 1 , 1 , 4 , 1 , 2 , 4 )    _____ - _____ = _____

**24.** ( 5 , 6 , 3 , -8 ) – ( 3 , 5 , 8 , - 5 )    _____ - _____ = _____

**25.** ( 6 , 5 , - 8 ) – ( -5 , 3 , -5 )    _____ - _____ = _____

# Mode Median Averages

Name _____   Date _____

**Directions**: Write the answer for each statement or question.

Given   ( 3 , 4 , 3 , 9 , 11 , 12 , 13 , 14 , 15 , 2 , 13 , 3 )

**1.** Find the mode, median, and average.

_____ , _____ , _____

**2.** Multiply the mode by the median. Then multiply by the average.

_____ X _____ X _____ = _____

**3.** Add the mode and median, then subtract the average.

_____ + _____ - _____ = _____

**4.** Measures of central tendency represent _____ values of a set of data.

**5.** If the numbers in a set of data are arranged in numerical order, then the _____ of the set is the middle number.

**6.** If all the numbers in a set of data occur the same number of times, then the set has no _____

**7.** Why do you think the mean, median, and modes are rarely the same value?

_____

_____

**8.** Define these words

**a.** Mode _____

_____

**b.** Median _____

_____

**c.** Average _____

_____

# Box and Whisker Plot

**Name** _____     **Date** _____

**Directions**: Find the errors in these box-and-whisker plots.

1.

2.

3.

4.

5.

6.

7.

```
0   10   20   30   40   50   60   70   80   90   100
```

Refer to problem 7 and answer questions 8 thru 12.

**8.** What is the range? _____

**9.** What is the median? _____

**10.** Name the lower extreme, lower quartile, median, and upper quartile.

**11.** Box-and Whisker plots are used to show _____ in data rather than specific numerical.

# Chapter 13

## Percentages

# Percentages 1

Name _____    Date _____

**Directions**: Match the problems with the answers. Place the numbers of the problems on the lines above the correct answers.

**1.** 27 is what percent of 36 ?

**2.** What percent of 48 is 30 ?

**3.** What percent of 26 is 30 ?

**4.** $ 12.50 is what percent of $ 7.50 ?

**5.** 9 is what percent of 20 ?

**6.** 9 is what percent of 10 ?

**7.** 4 is what percent of 50 ?

**8.** What percent of 50 is 15 ?

**9.** 60 is what percent of 12 ?

**10.** 1/3 is what percent of ¼ ?

| A | B | C | D |
|---|---|---|---|
| ____ | ____ | ____ | ____ |
| 45 % | 3 % | 30 % | .3 % |

| E | F | G | H |
|---|---|---|---|
| ____ | ____ | ____ | ____ |
| 133 1/3 % | 500 % | 40 % | 20 % |

| I | J | K | L |
|---|---|---|---|
| ____ | ____ | ____ | ____ |
| 75 % | 59 % | 95 % | 62.5 % |

| M | N | p | Q |
|---|---|---|---|
| ____ | ____ | ____ | ____ |
| 166 % | 8 % | 115.4 % | 90 % |

# Percentages 2

Name _____    Date _____

**Directions**: Match each answer with the correct problem. Write the letter of each correct answer in the correct box.

| | | | |
|---|---|---|---|
| 16 is 5 % of what number? | **27**  A | 4 % of what number is 12? | **3.92**  B  25 is 10 % of what number? |
| **92**  C | 35 is 200 % of what number? | **166.67**  D | 18 is 1 2/3 % of what number?  **249.75**  E |
| 18 is 40 % of what number? | **2500**  F | 15 % of 180 is what number? | **17.50**  G  23 is 25 % of what number? |
| **2837.14**  H | 135 % of 185 is what number? | **250**  I | 8 is 5 % of what number?  **160**  J |
| 43 % of 6,598 is what number? | **1080**  K | 8 % of what number is 200? | **320**  L  14 % of 28 is what number? |
| **300**  T | 5 is 30 % of what number? | **45**  W | 5 is 3 % of what number?  5     16.67 |

202

# Chapter 14

## Circle Graphs

# Circle Graph 1

Name _____     Date _____

**Directions**: Draw a circle graph to determine the given answers. Use your own paper.

**1ˢᵗ Qtr. George 50 Students**     **2ʳᵈ Qtr. Beth 20 Students**
**3ʳᵈ Qtr. Sam 20 Students**      **4ᵗʰ Qtr. Dennis 10 Students**

1. What is the total number of students?

2. What is the percentage of students in each class?

3. How many students are in Mr. Jones class?

4. What is the average number of students in a class?

5. Give a title for the circle.

6. What is the mode?

7. What is the median?

8. What is the ratio for George and Dennis?

9. What is the ratio for Beth and Sam?

10. What is the ratio for Dennis and Sam?

11. What is the greater ratio in numbers 9 and 10?

12. Change numbers 9 and 10 to two decimals and add the two decimals.

13. What is three percent of the mode?

14. Add the mode and the median.

# ANSWERS TO ALGEBRA 1 ACTIVITIES

+  Plus , increased , total , more , add
−  Minus , less , decreased ,subtract
X  Times , of , multiply , double , product
/  Divided by , quotient

**Use parentheses with sum of, difference of, product of, quotient of**

**Reverse the number and variable with more than and less than**

| Example 1 | Example 2 | Example 3 | Example 4 | Example 5 | Example 6 |
|---|---|---|---|---|---|
| 4 more than 3 | 5 less than 7 | 5 increased by 20 | 8 increased by 4 | 3 times 5 | 2 subtract From 20 |
| 3 + 4 | 7 − 5 | 5 + 20 | 8 + 4 | 3X5 | 20 − 2 |

## Verbal Expressions 1

1 (A), 20 (B), 8 (C), 5 (D), 19 (E)

3 (F), 18 (G), 2 (H), 4 (I), 6 (J), 16 (K)

22 (L), 15 (M), 17 (N), 14 (O), 7 (P), 13 (Q)

9 (R), 21 (S), 10 (T), 11 (U), 12 (V)

## Verbal Expressions 2

1.) $X^5$ 2.) (5X) 3.) $5 + 2X$ 4.) $1/5X^2$ 5.) 5x

6.) $3 (5 − X^3)$ 7.) $5 + 3X$ 8.) $5 + X$ 9.) $X − 5$ 10.) $5/X$

11.) $5 + 5X^2$ 12.) $5 − 2X$ 13.) 5 (4X) 14.) $5X - X$

15.) $5 + 4X$ 16. ) $5^2$ 17.) $-5X$ 18.) (3 (5X) )19 $X^5 + X$

## Verbal Expressions 3

1.) A= 2 +3 2.) M= 3− 4.) 3). B= (4x4) 4.) N= 8 /4

5.) C= 5 +2 6.) O= 3 + 5 7.) D=5x3 8.) P = 6 /7

9.) E= 5 − 4 10.) Q= 8 -7 11.) F= 6 + 7 12.) R=(6 − 4)

13.) G= 6/3 14.) S= 5(4) 15.) H= (3 /7) 16.) T= 5 -3

17.) I= 3 − 5 18.) U= 2 + 4 19.) J = = 5x2 20.) V (3 + 5)

21.) K= 4 /5 22.) W= 9 + 3 23.) L= 6 - 5

## Box and Key 4

1.) D 2.) P 3.) F 4.) T 5.) O

6.) GorJ 7.) H 8.) E 9.) L 10.) I

11.) N 12.) U 13.) A 14.) K

15.) J or G 16.) A

## Algebraic Expressions

Substitute in the algebraic expression to determine the answers. Given a=2 ,b= -4, c=1/2, e=2.1, f=.007, and d = 2 2/3.

| Example 1 | Example 2 | Example 3 | Example 4 | Example 5 |
|---|---|---|---|---|
| a + b + c | a b f | cd | d / c | f / e |
| (2+-4)+.5 | (2)(-4)(.007) | 1 /2 (2 2/3) | 2 2/3 ÷ ½ | .007 ÷2.1 |
| -2 + .5 | (-8)(.007) | ½ 8/3 | 8/3÷ (1 /2) | .00333 |
| -1.5 | -.056 | 1 /2 (8/3) | 16/3 | |
| | | 1.33 | 5  1/3 | |

### Magic Picture 1

1.) a 1384 2.)b 1257.5 3.) c 173.5 4.)d 854
5.) e 137.94 6.) f 5 5/6 7.) g 3 5/6 8.) h 1 1/ 6
9.) i 230,920 10.) j 150,600 11.) k 5405 12.) L) 8.17
13.) m 1 1/6 14.) n 1 1 /2 15.) O 2 /3 16.) p 2/21
17.) q 50 18.) r 1225 19.) s 138.4 20.) t 22500
21.) u76.67 22.) v 774 23.) w 1234 24.) x 1/27
25.) y7.83

### Algebraic Expression 2

A=5,B=25,C=22,D=.0004
E.=1,F=1.5,G=18.9,H=6
I=40, J=5,K=19.6,L=.066

### Algebraic Expression 3

$2a+b=L$
$a+b=2.3$
$j/b=E$
$bf+e=B$
$5c-d=J$
$c/i=D , c-j=D , b/f+b=K$
$fj+e=Z, a^2+b=G$

### Properties of Real Numbers

| Reflexive Property | Property of Zero | Additive Identity | Symmetry Property |
|---|---|---|---|
| 6 = 6 | 6 X 0 = 0 | 6 + 0 = 6 | If 6 = 5 +1,Then 5 + 1 = 6 |

| Distributive Property | Commutative Property for multiplication | Additive Inverse |
|---|---|---|
| 3( 6 + 2 ) = 18 + 6 | 7 X 9 = 9 X 7 | 6 + - 6 = 0 |

| Substitution Property | Associative Property for multiplication | Transitive Property |
|---|---|---|
| ( 3 + 2 ) + 7 = 5 + 7 | ( 3 x2) 5 = 3 (2 x 5 ) | If 6 = 2 + 4 and 2 + 4 = 3 + 3, Then 6 = 3 + 3 |

| Multiplicative Identity | Commutative Property for Addition | Associative Property for Addition |
|---|---|---|
| 7x 1 = 1 | 7 + 8 = 8 + 7 | (5 + 7)+ 10= 5 +(7 + 10) |

# Properties of Real Numbers 1

1. A 40=40          2. B 4X0=0          3. C NG          4. D If 1+2=3,then 3=1+2          5. E 2(5+3)=10+6
6. F 2x3=3x2          7. G NG          8. H 2x1=2          9. I 3+(5+2)=(3+5)+2          10. J 2+1=1+2
11. K (2x3)5 =2(3x5)  12. L 1+(3+2) = 1+ 5          13. M NG          14. N 2 + -2 = 0          15. O 6 X 1/6=1

# Properties of Real Numbers 2

A =1, B = 5, C = 3, D = 11, E = 10, F = 7, G = 6, H = 2, I  NG, J = 4, K = 12, L = 8, M = 9

# Properties of Real Numbers 3

1. H    2. C    3. G    4. Not Given    5. K    6. O    7. I    8. B    9. L    10. J    11. M    12. A    13. F

# Properties of Real Numbers 4

1. Additive Identity          2. Multiplicative Inverse          3. Multiplicative Identity
4. Property of Zero          5. Symmetry Property          6. Additive Inverse
7. Transitive Property          8. Substitution Property          9. Reflexive Property
10. Distributive Property          11. Associative for Addition          12. Commutative for Addition
13. Additive Identity          14. Multiplicative Identity          15. Reflexive Property
16. Property of Zero          17. Substitution Property          18. Reflexive Property
19. Multiplicative Identity          20. Distributive Property

# Properties of Real Numbers 5

1. Yes          2. Yes          3. Yes          4. NO          5. NO          6. Yes          7. Yes          8. NO
9. NO          10. Yes          11. Yes          12. Yes          13. Yes          14. NO          15. NO

# Adding and Subtracting integers and Rational Numbers

|                  ADDING                  |                  SUBTRACTING                  |
| :--- | :--- |
| Positive 6 and Positive 4 = Positive 10 | (Positive 8) - (Positive 4) = Positive 4 |
| Negative 6 and Negative 4= Negative 10 | (Negative 9) - (Negative 7) = Negative 2 |
| Positive 8 and Negative 14 = Negative 6 | (Positive 6) - (Negative 3) = Positive 9 |
| Positive 20 and Negative 10 = Positive 10 | Negative 20 –(Positive 15) = Negative 35 |

When adding a positive number and a negative number , subtract and use the sign of the greater number.

When subtracting two numbers, change the number inside the parentheses to the opposite sign, then add.

| Example 1 | Example 2 | Example 3 | Example 4 | Example 5 | Example 6 |
| :---: | :---: | :---: | :---: | :---: | :---: |
| 5 + 7 | 6 - (8) | -6 + -6 | 7 - (- 5) | 13 + -7 | -5 –(-4) |
| 12 | 6+-8 | -12 | 7+ 5 | 6 | -5 + 4 |
|  | -2 |  | 12 |  | -1 |

## Adding Integers 1

1. Golf (18)   2. My(-14)   3. Tiger(13)   4. Best (3)   5. Basic (9)   6. Digest (18)

7. Rage (9)   8. Tall (2)   9. Citizen (6)   10. Little (10)   11. Travel (-7)   12. James (-3)

13. Raymond (-11)   14. Portable (6)   15. Jackson (-8)   16. Amazing (5)   17. Technology (10)

18. Adding Integers (28)

## Adding Integers and Rational Numbers 2

1. (-4)   2. (-10)   3. (-4)   4. (-12)   5. (-10)   6. (-8)

7. (7)   8. (-9)   9. (-1)   10. (-9)   11. (-11)   12. (-3)

13. (4)   14. (-11.0)   15. (12)   16. (8)   17. (7)   18. (-9)

19. (3)   20. (5)

## Adding Integers 3

1). 7 and -5 = 2    2). -5 and 4 = -1    3). -5 and -4 = -9    4). 5 and 6 = 11    5). 10

6). 3    7). -13    8). -10    9). -11    10). -11

11). -8    12). 1    13). -19    14). -1

## Adding Integers 4

WIZARD'S 102    Max'S -341    The winner of the game is Wizard.

## Adding Integers 5

1). -10    2). -2    3). -3    4). -6    5). -22    6). -62    7). -67    8). 59    9).-11    10). 9    11). 74    12). -92

## Adding Integers 6

1. A&D    2. B & T    3. C & U    4. D & A    5. E & F    6. F & E    7. L &K    8. J &R    9. N & S

## Adding  Integers 7

1). 20    2). 7    3). -5    4). 3    5). 11    6). -20    7). -14    8). -16    9). 20    10). 1 7    11). 51    12). 6    13). 85

14). 15    15). 55    16). -21    17). 9    18). 47    19). 1    20). 16    21). -24    22). 41    23). -7

## Adding Integers 8

1. ABCF 8    2. AGHWA -112    3. HDWG -75    4. GHDI -64    5. GABCW -41

6. HDWAB -15    7. DWFCA 2    8. AWDIG 166    9. IHGWA -72    10. GHDWA -77

## Adding Integers 9

1.) Blue -3    2.) Tan -13    3.) Purple 25    4.) Blue -24    5.) Red 5    6.) Orange -16

7.) Brown 26    8.) Blue -15    9.) Pink -17    10.) green 45    11.) Yellow -11    12.) Gray 6

13.) Black -7    14.) Brown -10    15.) Green -14    16.) Yellow 14    17. Red 86

## Adding Integers 10

1.) 2   2.) -9   3.) -13   4.) 11   5.) 9   6.) -6   7.) -1`   8.) 1   9.) -11   10.) -4   11.) 21   12.) 19
13.) 0   14.) 8   15.) -16   16.) -7   17.) 7   18.) 3   19.) -5   20.) -15

## Adding Integers 11

Group A 1106          Group B 33,267          Total 34,373

## Adding Integers 12

| January | | | | | | | February | | | | | | | March | | | | | |
|---|---|---|---|---|---|---|---|---|---|---|---|---|---|---|---|---|---|---|---|
| Total | | | | | | | Total | | | | | | | Total | | | | | |
| -29 | | | | | | | -29 | | | | | | | 628 | | | | | |
| -45 | | | | | | | -46 | | | | | | | 555 | | | | | |
| 16 | | | | | | | -77 | | | | | | | 235 | | | | | |
| -5 | 2 | -2 | -17 | -10 | -26 | -58 | -5 | 2 | -2 | -18 | -65 | -64 | -152 | 300 | -235 | -1442 | 547 | 124 | 1879 |
| S | M | T | W | TH | F | | S | M | T | W | TH | F | | S | M | T | W | TH | F |

(1183)

## Adding Integers and Rational Numbers 1

1. -684.56   2. -656.991   3. -648.941   4. -46.28   5. 15.676   6. 29.49
7. -115.56   8. 5.72

## Subtracting Integers 1

1.) -1   2.) 0   3.) -1   4.) 63   5.) -16   6.) -16   7.) 56   8.) 14   9.) 4   10.) 15   11.) 3
12.) 28   13.) 4   14.) 4   15.) 27   16.) -10   17.) 17   18.) 1   19.) 7   20.) 8

## Subtracting Integers 2

1) 6005   2) 5515   3) 716   4) 4562   5) -6089   6) -111   7) 645   8) -1086   9) -445   10) 0
11) 10113   12) -15357   13) 2721   14) 197   15) -1308

## Subtracting Integers 3

1. Y        2. N        3. N        4. Y        5. Y        6. Y        7. Y        8. Y        9. N

10. N        11. Y        12. Y        13. N        14. Y        15. Y        16. N        17. N        18. N

## Subtracting Integers 4

1). H-L=91 −(-43) = 134    2.) B−D    23        3). K−F    -190        4.) N−A    -145        5). G−B    -304

6.) D−F    -4        7.) H−N    142        8.) L−D    -147        9). A−N    145        10.) H−F    -17

11). A−C    141        12.) D−A    10        13.) C−F    -155        14.) B−K    209

## Subtracting Integers 5

12 -6 = 6 +3 = 9 -3 = 6 -5 = 1 +6 = 7 -5 = 2 +4 = 6 -8 = -2 -2 = -4 -20 = -24 +6 = -18-4 = -22

+5 = -17-30 = -47

## Subtracting Integers 6

1.) A −B -1        2.) B − C 7        3.) C − D 2        4.) D − E -13        5.) E − F 12

6.) F -G 6        7.) G −A -13        8.) G − C -7        9.) G −D -5        10.) G − G 0

11.) G −F -6        12.) G − B -14        13.) C-A -6        14.) E − G 18        15.) D −F -1

16.) F −A -7        17.) F −B +2 -6        18.) F-B -8        19.) E −B 4        20.) G − B -14

## Subtracting Integers and Rational Numbers 7

1. $ 10.84        2. $ .46        3. $ 39.01        4. G  -1 = -6.18    5. $ -130.62        6. $ 218.87

7. $ 21.31        8. $ 67.15        9. $ -41.11        10. $ -49.78        11. $ 5.24        12. $ 27.85

13. $ 79.63        14.$ -3.36        15. $ 39.01        16. $ 19.13        17. $ -23.55        18. $ -159.94

# Multiplication and Division of Integers and Rational Numbers
## Multiplication and division rules are the same.

### Multiplication
1. Positive times Positive = Positive
2. Negative times Negative = Positive
3. Positive times Negative = Negative
4. Negative times Positive = Negative
5. $8 \times 4\ 3/6 = 8/1 \times 27/6 = 4/1 \times 27/3 = 36$

### Division
1. Positive divided by Positive = Positive
2. Negative divided by Negative = Positive
3. Positive divided by Negative = Negative
4. Negative divided by Positive = Negative
5. $5\ 2/4 \div 1\ 2/3 = 22/4 \div 5/3 = 22/4 \times 3/5 = 66/20 = 33/10 = 3\ 3/10$

## Multiplying Integers 1

| | | | | | | |
|---|---|---|---|---|---|---|
| 1.) -16 | 2.) 12 | 3.) -27 | 4.) 4 | 5.) 24 | 6.) 28 | 7.) 27 |
| 8.) -54 | 9.) -6 | 10.) 40 | 11.) -34 | 12.) 22 | 13.) 0 | 14.) 32 |
| 15.) 75 | 16.) -24 | 17.) -12 | 18.) 25 | 19.) -81 | 20.) 30 | 21.) 72 |
| 22. -16 | | | | | | |

## Multiplying Integers 2

| | | | | | |
|---|---|---|---|---|---|
| 1.) 48 | 2.) -30 | 3.) 24 | 4.) -12 | 5.) 42 | 6.) -60 |
| 7.) 144 | 8.) -4 | 9.) 0 | 10.) 3 | 11.) -240 | 12.) -8 |
| 13.) -16 | 14.) 34 | 15.) 14 | 16.) -121 | 17.) -630 | 18.) 126 |

## Multiply Integers 3

| | | |
|---|---|---|
| 1. Jack went to Illinois | 2. Bill went to Maryland | 3. Mary went to Michigan |
| 4. Bob went to Maine | 5. Jerry went to Ohio | 6. Tom went New York |
| 7. Alt went to Colorado | 8. Jan went to Georgia | 9. Bird went to Texas |
| 10. Tim went to North Carolina | 11. Jim went to Kansas | 12. Will went to Virginia |
| 13. Ted went to Connecticut | 14. Bull went to Rhode Island | 15. Todd went nowhere |
| 16. Can went to Indiana | 17. Shell went to California | 18. Paul went to Hawaii |

## Multiplying Integers 4

| | | | | | | | | | |
|---|---|---|---|---|---|---|---|---|---|
| 1. B | 2. D | 3. E | 4. I | 5. K | 6. M | 7. S | 8. U | 9. P | 10. G |
| 11. R | 12. Q | 13. H | 14. O | 15. F | 16. T | 17. N | 18. J | 19. L | 20. G |
| 21. K | 22. C | 23. Z | 24. V | 25. $B_1$ | 26. X | 27. W | 28. $A_1$ | 29. Y | |

# Multiplying Integers 5

Remove all of the rectangles and put them in order

# Multiplying Integers 6

A. -32     B. 192     C. 144     D. -46     E. -132     F. -64     G. 108     H. 184     I. 152     J. 86
K. 188     L. 0     M. -150     N. 144     O. 174     P. 174     Q. 195     R. -140

# Multiplying Integers 7

1.) 12     2.) -24     3.) 1     4.) 27     5.) -32     6.) -140     7.) -64     8.) 12     9.) 42     10.) -36
11.) 40     12.) 6     13.) -24     14.) 64     15.) -30     16.) 30     17.) 24     18.) 0     19.) 12     20.) 12

# Multiplying and Dividing Rational Numbers 8

1. NG     2. NG     3. Ball     4. NG     5. NG     6. Cup     7. Glass     8. Box
9. Cone     10. Hat     11. NG     12. Pen     13. Cylinder     14. Watch     15. Ring     16. Boat

# Multiplying Integers and Rational Numbers 9

The students can select any two or three numbers.
1. AB = -9          2. BC = 17          3.CD = -24 5/9          4. DE = -11 5/9          5. EF = 8/9
6. FG = 1          7. GH = 3          8. HI = ¾          9. IJ = -6 3/4          10. JC = -51
11. DE = -11.5          12. AK = 4.5          13. IE = 2          14. A F = --1          15. FK = -1/2
16. AH. -3          17. AI = -2.25          18. CI = 4 1/4          19. BD = -13          20. FE = 8/9
21. BF = 1          22. BG = 9          23. BH = 3          24. BI = 2.25          25. BJ = -27

# Multiplying Integers and Rational Numbers 10

1.) 112          2.) -622,080     3.) 528          4.) -48          5.) -131.625     6.) -189          7.) 0

## Dividing Integers and Rational Numbers 1

1.) -36   2.) 36   3.) 1   4.) -1   5.) 2   6.) -2   7.) 2   8.) -2   9.) 1   10.) -1   11.) 1 ¼
12.) -1   13.) 3   14.) 2   15.) -36   16.) 16   17.) -16   18.) 0   19.) -2   20.) -18   21.) -36

## Dividing Integers and Rational Numbers 2

1. A   2. D   3. H   4. F   5. M   6. L   7. J   8. N   9. K   10. G   11. I   12. E   13. C   14. B

## Dividing Integers and Rational Number 3

1. A   2. J   3. R   4. H   5. G.   6. C   7. F   8. Q   9. I   10. N   11. M   12. E
13. K   14. L   15. P.   16. O   17. B   18. D

## Dividing Integers and Rational Numbers 4

Remove all of the rectangles and put them in order

## Dividing Integers and Rational Numbers 5

4.1   -22.5   -40   .606   -1 13/20   4 1/11   -60   -1 1/10   7/8   -7 1/3   13/24   3 6/7

## Adding, Subtracting, Multiplying and Dividing Fractions

1. 1 1/6   2. -7 /24   3. 5 /12   4. 3 /4   5. 4 /a   6. $(a - 14)/ 2a^2$   7. $1 / A^8 B^5 C^8$
8. $9 a^3/ 20b^3$   9. $1 /2B^2$   10. $(a - b)^2/(a + b)^4$   11. $( 3a + 2 ) / ( a + 2 )^2$
12. $4b + 3a^4/ 6a^3 b$   13. $1 / ( a + b )^2$   14. $a/ 2(a - 1)$

## Order of Operations

**There are six steps in order of operations.**

| | |
|---|---|
| **1. Write the problem** | $120 - (2 + 1)^2 \times 4 / 6$ |
| **2. Do the operation inside parentheses, brackets, fractions bars.** | $120 - (3)^2 \times 4 / 6$ |
| **3. Do all your powers** | $120 - 9 \times 4 / 6$ |
| **4. Do all multiplications and divisions from left to right. L to R** | $120 - 36 / 6$ |
| | $120 - 6$ |
| **5. Do additions and subtractions from left to right.** | $114$ |

## Order of Operations 1

Create examples using addition signs (+), Multiplication signs (X), and parentheses (  ) between 2, 8, 3 and 4. Show your work. Answers will vary

Example

( 2  x  8  +  3  x  4  )

(     16    +    12      )

28

## Order of Operations 2

Create examples using addition (+) or subtraction (-) signs between 2, 8, 3, and 4.
Use parentheses ( ) in all examples. Show your work. Answers will vary.

Example

( 2 + 8 − 3 ) + 4

(10 +-3) + 4

7 + 4

11

## Order of Operations 3

Solve these problems by using addition (+), subtraction (-), and multiplication (X) signs between 2, 8, 3, and -3. Use parentheses in all problems. Answers will vary.

**Example**

**4 ( 2 + 8 - 3 )**

**4 ( 10 + -3 )**

**4( 7 )**

**28**

## Order of Operations 5

(A)    Given   Parentheses   Power   Multiplication   Divide   Add   Answer

(B)    Given   Parentheses Power   Multiply from L to R   Multiply from L to R   Divide   Answer

(C)    Given   Parentheses   Multiply from L to R   Multiply from L to R   Divide   Answer

(D)    Given   Multiply from L to R   Add from L to R   Add from L to R   Answer

(E)    Given   Parentheses   Multiply from L to R   Subtract   Answer

(F)    Given   Power   Divide from L to R   Multiply   Subtract   Answer

(G)    Given   Parentheses   Powers   Add from L to R   Add   Answers

## Order of Operations 6

A is correct.

B is incorrect.

$$24 + 8 / 8 = 24 + 1 = 25$$

C is incorrect.

$$2 \times 8 = 16 , 8 + 16 - 10 + 8$$
$$24 - 10 + 8$$
$$14 + 8$$
$$22$$

D is incorrect.

$$-91$$

E is incorrect. Multiply before you add

$$(2 \times 5 + 4 + -8)/2$$
$$(10 + 4 + -8)/2$$
$$(14 + -8)/2$$
$$6 / 2 = 3$$

F is incorrect.

$$8 + 2 = 10$$

G is incorrect. An extra 2 is in the problem.

$$1/2(4 - 2)3/3$$
$$1/2 \times 2 \times 3/3$$
$$1 \times 3/3$$
$$3 /3 = 1$$

H is incorrect.

$$2 \times 216 \times 4/2$$
$$432 \times 4/2$$
$$1728/2$$
$$864$$

## Order of Operations 7

(1) A  C  B    (2) A  C  D  B    (3) A  D  C  B    (4) A  C  E  B  D    (5) A  D  C  B

## Order of Operations 8

1) 57.5    2) 27    3) 100    4) 480    5) 80    6) 20    7) 75    8) 30

9) 100    10) 108

## Order of Operations 9

1) G     2) V     3) H     4) B bv     5) V     6) E     7) I     8) A     9) C     10) J

## Order of Operations 10

Bedroom 2 (35) Bedroom 3 (7) Library (102) Family Room (15) Theater (11) Linen closet (80) Kitchen (53) Dining Room (6) Sunroom (10) Porch (1)

## Equations

### Solving Equations

1. $-x = 4$
$-1 / -1x = 4 / -1$
$x = -4$

2. $2x = 4$
$2/2x = 4/2$
$x = 2$

3. $1/3x = 2$
$(3)1/3 \, x = 2(3)$
$x = 6$

4. $3x = 2 \frac{1}{4}$
$3x = 2 \frac{1}{4}$
$3x = 9/4$
$1/3(3)x = 9/4 \times 1/3$
$x = \frac{3}{4}$

5. $X + 3.7 = 8$
$X + 3.7 = 8$
$-3.7 = -3.7$
$x = 4.3$

6. $2x - 7 = -8$
$+7 = 7$
$2x = -1$
$\frac{1}{2}(2x) = -1(1/2)$
$x = -1/2$

7. $3x + 2 = 5x - 8$
$-2 = -2$
$3x = 5x - 10$
$-5x = -5x$
$-2x = -10$
$X = 5$

8. $2/3(x + 3) = 8$
$2/3X + 2 = 8$
$-2 = -2$
$2/3x = 6$
$3/2(2/3x) = 3/2 (6)$
$x = 9$

9. $1 1/2 (x + 3) = 2/3(X - 2)$
$1 1/2x + 3/2 = 2 1/3x - 4 1/3$
$6(1/2 x + 3/2 = 2/3x - 4/3)$
$3x + 9 = 4x - 8$
$-9 = -9$
$3x = 4x - 17$
$-4x \quad -4x$
$-x = -17$
$X = 17$

10. $x/3 + 3/6 = 2/4 + 1/2$
$12 (x/3 + 3/6 = 2/4 + 1/2)$
$4x + 6 = 6 + 6$
$4x + 6 = 12$
$-6 = -6$
$4x = 6$
$\frac{1}{4}(4x) = \frac{1}{4}(6)$
$x = 6/4 = 1 1/2$

## Equations 1

1) 5in.    2) ½ in.    3) 5 in.    4) ¼ in.    5) 5 ¼in.    6) 3 in.    7) 1/8 in.

8) 2 in.    9) 5 in.    10) 1 in.    11) 3 in.    12) 4in.    13) 0in.    14) 6in.

15) 3in.    16) 1in.    17) 0 in.    18) 5 in.    19) 6in.    20) 3.5 in.    21) 5 in.

22) 3 ½ in.    23) 2 ½ in.    24) 4 ¼ in.    25) 6 7/8in.    26) 4.5 in.

## Equations 2

A) Yes    B) Yes    C) No    D) No    E) Yes    F) No    G) Yes    H) Yes    I) Yes    J) Yes

K) No    L) Yes    M) Yes    N) Yes    O) No    P) Yes    Q) No

## Equations or Formulas 3

1. Solve for A    $A = (-2B + C)/2$    2. Solve for F    $F = 9/5C + 32$

3. Solve for r    $R = c/6.28$    4. Solve for H    $H = 2C/B$

5. Solve for r    $r = \sqrt{c}/3.14H$    6. Solve for $b_1$    $b_1 = 2C/h - b^2$

7. Solve for W    $W = C/LH$    8. Solve for r    $r = C/t$

9. Solve for r    $r = \sqrt{3}C/3.14$    10. Solve for x    $x = 3/2C - 12$

11. Solve for r    $r = (C - 2B)/6.28h$

## Equations 4

1) 2    2) -2    3) 4.5    4) -1    5) -1 1/6    6) 8 1/6    7) -1    8) 2.4    9) 6 28/45    10) 4 11/15

11) 7/8    12) - 6 ¼    13) 13 .5    14) -1.4    15) 2/3    16) 5.5    17) .4    18) -106    19) 3.10    20) -17 ¾

## Equations 5

| 6 | -6 | -18 | 18 | 2 4/7 | -2 4/7 | -6 /7 | 6 /7 |
|---|----|-----|----|-------|--------|-------|------|
| 2 | 6  | 3   | 1  | 3     | 2      | 2     | 1    |

## Equations 6

5 2/3    12    -21    6    9.6    1    12    6.8    9    3 1/5

## Equations 7

1. 3        2. -4        3. -12        4. 2        5. 1/6        6. 2/7        7. 18 8/22        8. -6 2/3

## Equations 8

FORD        DODGE        AVALON        SONATA

## Equations 9

**1. 3        2. -3        3. -46        4. 71        5. 0        6. -1/12**

## Equations 10

1. 1        2. -1/18

## Equations 11

1. -10        2. 2

## Equations 12

| | | | | | | |
|---|---|---|---|---|---|---|
| Tan 24 | Yellow 40 | Blue -191 | Red 10 | Green 6 | Purple 0 | Orange 259 |
| Purple 0 | Black 60 | Red -12 2/3 | Red 7.5 | Green -10 | Blue 250 | |

## Inequalities

In solving inequalities problems, change the inequality sign when we multiply by a negative number or divide by a negative number.

**1.** $-6x + 3 \leq 2x - 4$
$-3 \leq -3$
$-6x \leq 2x - 7$
$-2x \leq -2x$
$-8x \leq -7$
$-8/-8x \leq -7/-8$
$x \geq 7/8$

**2.** $-2/3\ x + 5 > 2x + 54$
$-5 > -5$
$-2/3\ x > 2x + 49$
$-2x > -2x$
$-2\ 2/3\ x > 49$
$-8/3x > 49$
$(-3/8)(-8/3)x > (-3/8)(49)$
$X < -18\ 3/8$

**3.** $3/5\ x + 2 \geq -5x - 3$
$-2 \geq -2$
$3/5x \geq -5x - 5$
$5x \geq +5x$
$5\ (3/5)\ x \geq -5$
$28/5x \geq -5$
$(5/28)(28/5)X \geq (5/28)(-5)$
$X \geq -25/28$

## Inequalities 1

1. A,C,G      2. A,B,G      3. A,E,G      4. A,D,G      5. A,D,G      6. A,A,D,G,G
7. A,A,D,G    8. A,C,C,G    9. A,D,C,E,G  10. A,F,B,D,G  11. A,F,C,C,E,G  12. A,C,C,E,G
13. A,D,C,C,G

## Inequalities 2

You can use letters from A to P to solve the rectangles

Left side   J,start,E,I,F,k,No  Answer,G        Right side   L,B,H,D,C,N,A,M

## Inequalities 3

1a.) c, d, g, f, b, e      2a.) r, c, s, d, g, e, b, t, k      3a.) h, f, j, i      4a.) c, t, h, k, y, f, d, g, w, e, b

## Inequalities 4

1a.) d , b , c        2a.) d , c , b        3a.) b , c , d        4a.) c , b
5a.) b                6a.) c , b            7a.) c , f , d , h ,e , g ,b.    8a.) d , c , b

# Inequalities 5

Left side x > 4 , x > 1/6 , x > -16 , x > 44 , Ø        Right side Ø , x>4.5 , x < -2 , All real no
        x < 3

# Inequalities 6 and Inequalities 7

Fun head and Vase

# Inequalities 8

1. X ≤ 3.003      2. x≤ 45       3. X < -7/10      4. X ≥ -8       5. X ≥ ¾       6. X ≤ 2
7. X ≥ 20         8. x > -2.752  9. X ≥ 176        10. X < -21 ½   11. X > -6.3   12. X ≤ 7 2/5
13. X ≥ 8 4/11    14. x ≤ -230   15. X < -26 2/3   16. X ≥ -5/13   17. All real numbers   18. x≤ 2
19. X < 4.3       20. x ≤ -2.8

# Inequalities 9

1. J≥ 50          2. J≤ 50       3. J < 7          4. J < 3        5. J ≤ 3       6. 6 + X > -2
7. (X-6)≥20       8. 3n> 2(n + 9)  9. 3n < 2( n + 9)   10. (3n + 9 ) < 2n   11. 3n≤ 36   12. N – (-4)≤2

# Graphing Absolute Values

1. X = 3 or X = -7        2. X = 0 or x = -2        3. X = 6 or x = -2        4. X ≥ 4 or x ≤ -1
5. x≤ 2 1/3 and x ≤1/3    6. X ≤ 2 and x ≥ -6       7. All real numbers       8. No answers
9. No solutions           10. X ≤ 3 and x≥ -3

## Laws of Exponents

1. $a^2a^3a^4 = a^{2+3+4} = a^9$    2. $2^3 \times 2^2 = 2^{3+2} = 2^5 = 32$    3. $(a^3b^2)^4 = a^{12}b^8$    4. $(2^2 \times 3^3)^2 = 2^4 \times 3^6$

$16 \times 729 = 11,664$    5. $A^6B^7 / A^5B^3 = (A^6/A^5)(B^7/B^3) = AB^4$

6. $A^5B^3C^7 / A^6B^5C^9 = (A^5/A^6)(B^3/B^5)(C^7/C^9) = (1/A)(1/B^2)(1/C^2) = 1/A^1B^2C^2$

## Laws of Exponents 1

1.) $100abc^4 = 32,400$    2.) $36,000/(ab) = 9,000.$    3.) $(ab)^6c = 139,968$    4.) $(abc)^4 = 20,736.$

5.) 2332.8    6.) 3840    7.) 65,536    8.) 16,384

9.) 72,900    10.) 248,832    11.) 3,691    12.) 186,624

13.) 196,608    14.) 12,288    15.) 187,656

## Laws of Exponents 2

A. $8a^6b^6c^9$    B. $32a^{15}b^{15}c^{20}$    C. $32a^{11}b^6$    D. $-32a^8b^{12}c^2$    E. $24a^7b^{15}c^8$    F. $1a^9b^{11}c^5$    G. $54a^9b^{11}c$

H. $1/32a^5b^5c^6$    I. $1a^7b^5c^4$    J. $6a^5b^7c^8$    K. $a^6b^4$    L. $0$    M. $1/2a^5b^5$    N. $-32a^{10}b^{15}c^{40}$

O. $\frac{1}{4}a^2b^2c^8$    P. $6a^2b^2c^2$

## Laws of Exponents 3

1.) Red 27    2.) Blue 1/27    3.) Red 64    4.) Red 1/8    5.) Yellow 81    6.) Yellow -1/125

7.) yellow 1    8.) Yellow 2.25    9.) Blue 10000    10.) Blue 1    11.) Blue 1000    12.) Blue 8

13.Green 1/16    14.) Green 12.7    15.) Green 1024    16.) Green 8/9    17.) Green 1/1024    18.) 1 1/3

## Laws of Exponents 4

1. S    2. P    3. D    4. Z    5. N    6. T    7. L    8. I    9. C    10. V

11. U    12. A    13. F    14. H    15. E    16. B    17. K    18. Q    19. Y    20. H

# Laws of Exponents 5

1.) $A^3$　2.) $A^6$　3.) $A^{11}$　4.) $A^{11}$　5.) $A^{17}$　6.) $A^{14}$　7.) $A^{12}$　8.) $A^{11}$　9.) $A^2$　10.) $A^{-7}$　11.) $A^6$　12.) $A^{-12}$

13.) $A^{-1}$　14.) $A^9$　15.) $A^{12}$　16.) $A^5$　17.) $A^3$　18.) $A^3$　19.) $A^{-6}$　20.) $A^5$　21.) $A^{12}$　22.) $A^{-4}$　23.) $A^4$　24.) $A^{18}$

25.) $A^6$　26.) $A^9$　27.) $A^{11}$　28.) $A^{15}$　29.) $A^{17}$　30.) $A^3$　31.) $A^{12}$　King Hat

# Laws of Exponents 6

1. Alice 1　　2. Sarah 6　　3. Al 160　　4. Mark 256　　5.Red 2　　6. Mel 2

7. Lou -1 1/7　8. Cat 288　9. Ned 256　10. Will 192　11. Me 6　12. Bill -3

# Laws of Exponents 7

1.) $a^2$　2.) $a^3b^2$　3.) $1/a^3b^3$　4.) $a^2b^2$　5.) $1/a^3b^4$　6.) $a^5b^3$　7.) $a^2b^3$　8.) $a^6b^4$　9.) 2

10.) 729　11.) $4y^2$　12.) $2x^{10}$　13.) $1/2x^3$　14.) $a^7b^5$　15.) $a^{11}b^{14}$　16.) $a^4b$　17.) $a^8b^{12}$　18.) 81

# Scientific Notations 1

1. W to B 370.34　2. 50110.34　　3. 70510.00041　4. 30,508.7　　5. 154008.702032

6. 166,824666.7　7. 30,008.702　8. 140620.34

# Scientific Notations 2

1. 99,000,000　2. 23.333　　3. 540　　4. 1,560,000　5. .000544　6. 34 ,500 ,000

7. 453 ,000　　8. 3000　　9. 450　　10. 1,590, 000　11. 987,000,000　12. 7,000

13. 02　　　　14. 6.756　15. 1

## Prime Factorization Numbers and Variables

**1.** $300a^5b^6c^2$ = 3 X 100 $a^5b^6c^2$ = 3 x 10 x 10 $a^5b^6c^2$ = 3 x 5x2 x5 x 2aaaaabbbbbbcc

**2.** 144 $a^3b^3$ = 12 x 12 =1x4x3x4x3 = 1x2x2x3x2x2x3 aaa bbb

## Prime Factorization Numbers and Variables 1

1.) = 1 2 2 2 a a b b b      2.) = 1 3 5 a b b b b      3.) = 1 2 2 5 a a a b b

4.) = 1 2 2 3 2 a a a b b b b b    5.) = 1 2 2 7 a a b b      6.) = 1 3 2 3 2 a a b b b

7.) = 1 3 2 7 a a a b b      8.) = 1 3 2 2 2 2 a b      9.) = 1 11 11 a a a a a a b b b b b

10.) = 1 5 5 5 a b      11.) = 1 5 5 7 a a a a b b b b      12.) = 1 3 3 3

13.) = 1 2 2 2 2 2 2 a      14.) = 13 3 3 3 aab bb b b      15.) = 1 7 2 2 2

16.) = 1 11 3 2 a a a      17.) = 1 3 2 2 5 2 a a a a a b      18.) = 1 5 5 2 a a a b b b b

19.) = 1 2 2 2 2 2 2 2 a b b b b b    20.) = 1 2 2 2 3 3 a a a a b b b

## Prime Factorizations 2

1. D      2. C      3. B      4. E      5. K      6. L      7. F      8. G      9. A      10. H

## Prime Factorizations 3

1.Red 1 2 2 2 2 2 5      2. Black -1 2 2 2 7 3 3      3. Pink-1 5 3 2 2 2 7 3      4. Orange -1 2 2 2 2

5. Tan 1 5 5 5 5 5      6. Blue 1 2 11 5 2      7. Brown 1 3 5 5 2      8. Yellow 1 2 2 2 3 3 3 3

9. Black 2 3 5 7 2      10. Tan -1 2 2 5 2 7      11. Yellow 1 2 2 37      12. Blue 1 2 3 29

13. Pink -1 5 2 5 2      14. Green 2 2 2 2 2 2      15. Tan 1 3 11 11      16.Orange -1 2 2 2 5 2 5 2

17. Green 1 2 3 5

## Prime Factorizations 4

D C A H B G F E J

## Greatest Common Factor

**Find the GCF for** $120\ a^2b^3$ **and** $200\ a^4b^6$

$120a^2b^3=12\times10=1\times4\times3\times5\times2aabb = 1\ \times\ 2\ \times\ 2\ \times\ 3\ \times\ 5\ \times\ 2\ a\ a\ b\ b\ b$

$200a^4b^6=2\times100=2\times10\times10 = 1\ \times\ 2\ \times\ 2\ \times\ 5\ \times\ 5\ \times\ 2\ a\ a\ a\ a\ b\ b\ b\ b\ b\ b$

**Write one term from each match.**            $1\times2\times2\times5\times2\ a\ a\ b\ b\ b\ =\ 40\ a^2b^3$

## Greatest Common Factor 1

1. The GCF for 20 and 48 is 4

2. The GCF for 24ab and 64ab is 8ab

3. The GCF for -45 and -72 is -9

4. The GCF for 120 and 140 is 20.

5. The GCF for -8, -12 and -32 is -4

6. The GCF for 36ab , 42ab , and 18ab is 6ab

7. The GCF for -56ab, 92ab is 4ab

8. The GCF for $81a^2b^3$ and $729a^3b^3$ is $81a^2b^3$

9. The GCF for $36a^3b^2$ , $12a^4b^3$ and $24a^3b^4$ is $12a^3b^2$

10. The GCF for $18a^3b$ , $20a^2b^2$, and $4a^3b^4$ is $2a^2b$.

## Greatest Common Factor 2

The GCF is . 6 , 8 , 2 , 11ab , 6 , 6a , $10a^2b^6c$ , $5a^3b^2$ , $10ab^2$

## Greatest Common Factor 3

1.) 120    2.) 3    3.) 2    4.) -21    5.) -3    6.) 210    7.) -1    8.) -15    9.) 3   10.)1

11.) 21    12.) 12    13.) 1    14.) 6    15.) -1    16.) 42    17.) 12

## Greatest Common Factor 4

1.). 4    2.) 16    3.) 25    4.) 2    5.) 1    6.) 2    7.) $14a^2b$    8.) $-6a^3b^3$    9.) $10\ a^3b^2$

10.) $b^3$    11.) $6a^3b^2$    12.) 50

## Greatest Common Factor 5

1.) 42       2.) 6       3.) 462       4.) 36       5.) 396       6.) -2       7.) 4       8.) 2       9.) 24
10.) 15       11.) 25       12.) 1

## Greatest Common Factor 6

-15   -10   -5   0   5   10   15   20   25   30   35   40   45   50   55   60   65   70   75   80

A = 4,       B = 12,       C = 6,       D = -12,       E = 54,       F = 22,       G = 13,       H = 3,
I = 24,       J = 15       K = 9,       L = 7,       M = 6,       N = 72,       O = 30

## Greatest Common Factor 7

1. $ABC( 1 + D )$

2. $A(BCD + BC + DER)$

3. $ABC(1+2D+DE)$

4. $ABC( 1 + D + DE + DEf)$

5. No GCF

6. $xxxx(xxx+2xx+1)$

7. $NUNN ( 1 + N + U )$

8. $Xux(2+xux+xx)$

9. $111111(i+1+111)$

## Multiplying Sums of Squares

1. $a^2 + 2ab + b^2$

2. $a^2 + 2ac + b^2$

3. $a^2 -2ab + b^2$

4. $A^2 + 2ab + b^2$

5. $4a^2 -4ab + b^2$

6. $9c^2 +12cB + 4B^2$

7. $4a^4 -12a^2c + 9c^2$

8. $16a^2 -8ab + b^2$

9. $4a^2 -12ab + 9b^2$

10. $16a^4+16a^2b+4b^2$

11. $a^4 + 8a^2b + 16 b^2$

12. $b^4 - 2b^4 + b^4 = 0$

13. $a^2 +4ac + 4c^2$

14. $a^2b^2 + 2ab^2 + b^2$

15. $0$

16. $c^2 + 2bc + b^2$

17. $a^2 -2ac + c^2$

18. $b^2 -2ab + a^2$

19. $9a^2 + 12ab + 4b^2$

20. $9b^2 + 24ab + 16a^2$

# Factoring Difference of Squares, Perfect Trinomials, and Trinomials

**Steps used to factor an expression**

1. Look for GCF.                                    1. Factor $2x^2 - 32$

2. GCF (terms)                                      2. $2(x^2 - 16)$

3. Try factoring the two terms inside the parentheses.    3. $2(x - 4)(x + 4)$

$X^2 + 2x + 1$                $x^2 - 2x + 1$                $x^2 + 3x - 4$

+    +    +                    +    -    +                   +    +    -


( + )( + )                     ( - )( - )                  ( + )( - ) or ( - )( + )

GCF (      )              next GCF (      )(        )    next GCF (      )(        )(        )

Next GCF (      )(      ) (      )(      )

---

**Example1**
$3x^2 + 9$
$3(x^2 + 3)$

**Example 2**
$3X^2 - 27$
$3(x^2 - 9)$
$3(x - 3)(x + 3)$

**Example 3**
$3x^3 + 12x^2 + 9x$
$3x(x^2 + 4x + 3)$
$3x(x + 1)(x + 3)$

**Example 4**
$3x^4 - 243$
$3(x^4 - 81)$
$3(x^2 - 9)(x^2 + 9)$
$3(x - 3)(x + 3)(x^2 + 9)$

**Example 5**
$3x^4 - 24x^2 + 48$
$3(x^4 - 8x^2 + 16)$
$3(x^2 - 4)(x^2 - 4)$
$3(x - 2)(x + 2)(x - 2)(x + 2)$

**Example 6**
$15x^2 - 3x - 18$
$3(5x^2 - x - 6)$
$3(5x - 6)(x + 1)$

**Example 7**
$15x^2 - 18x + 15x - 18$
$(15x^2 + 15x) + (-18x - 18)$
$15x(x + 1) - 18(x + 1)$
$(x + 1)(15x - 18)$
$(15x - 18)(x + 1)$
$3(5x - 6)(x + 1)$

**Example 8**
$15x^2 + 15x - 18x - 18$
$3[5x^2 + 5x - 6x - 6]$
$3[(5x^2 + 5x) + (-6x - 6)]$
$3[5x(x + 1) - 6(x + 1)]$
$3[(x + 1)(5x - 6)]$
$3(x + 1)(5x - 6)$

## Sum and Differences of Two Cubes

$$A^3 + B^3 = (A + B)(A^2 - AB + B^2) ; A^3 - B^3 = (A - B)(A^2 + AB + B^2)$$

1. C,D,H,P    2. M  G  Q    3. Not given   4. N       5. J       6. B       7. 0
8. I          9. E          10. Not given  11. R      12. L      13. M

## Trinomials 1

1. No Answer        2. (7x - 1)(3x − 2)   3. No answer      4. No answer      5. (3x − 4)(x + 2)
6.. (x + 2)(x + 3)   7. (x + 1)(x + 5)     8. (x + 1)(x + 1)  9. (3x + 1)(x - 4)
10. 2(3x -1) (6x + 1)   11. (3x − 4)(x + 1)   12. (3x -4) (2x + 3)   13. No answer

## Trinomials 2

1. H    2. X    3. A or I   4. D    5. Q    6. F    7. T    8. A or I   9. E    10. C   11. W   12. J   13. S

## Trinomials 3

9 x 5 3 1 x 2 8 6 7 0 4 6

## Trinomials 4

Left side of the tree          12, 13, 7, 17, 1, 15

Middle part of the tree        8 -- 18, 9

Right side of the tree         6, 2, 3, 10, 16, 14

# Quadratic Equations

**Middle term**
$\downarrow$

Factor $x^2 + 3x + 1$        Factor the problem and check it
    ( x + 1 )( x + 1 )        Check your problem        1x + 1x does not equal 3x.
If you do not get the middle term, use the quadratic formula.

$$X = ( -b \pm \sqrt{(b^2 - 4ac)}/ 2a$$

Factor $x^2 + 3x + 1$    a = 1 , b = 3 , c = 1        $x = ( -3 \pm \sqrt{(3^2 - 4(1)(1))} / 2(1)$

$$X = ( -3 \pm \sqrt{(9 - 4)}/2$$
$$X = ( -3 \pm \sqrt{5} ) /2$$
$$X = (-3 \pm \sqrt{5} )/ 2$$

## Quadratic Equations 1

| | | | | |
|---|---|---|---|---|
| A. (0,4) | B. (0,-6) | C. (2,-2) | D .(0,-2.5) | E. (4,-4) |
| F. (-1,-1) | G. (0,-6 2/3) | H. (7/8,1 2/3) | I. (4,4) | J. (-1/ 2 ,-1/3) |
| K.($\pm$2.4, $\pm$ i$\sqrt{6}$) | L. (1 1/3 ,-4) | M. (-7 ,7) | N. (0,-5,5) | O. ($\pm$2, 2) |
| P. (1/3 , -3 ½) | Q. (-6,-2) | R. ($\pm$3,$\pm$2) | S. (0,-3,-2) | T. (-8,4) |

## Quadratic Equations 2

| | | | | |
|---|---|---|---|---|
| A.) 3.19,.139 | B.) .75 , -1 | C.) 1 2/3 , -2 | D.) 3$\pm$2.65i | E.) -8.5 ,3 |
| F.) $\pm$9.90 | G.) (3$\pm$17.78i)$\div$2 | H.) 4.08 ,-2.575 | I.) 13.545 , -3.545 | J.) .468 , -2.135 |
| K.) $\pm$3.16 | L.) 2.825,-.825 | M.) 0 ,-4 ,2 | N.) $\pm$ 6 | O.) 0 ,8 |

## Quadratic Equations 3

| | | | | |
|---|---|---|---|---|
| A.) ( 1$\pm$i$\sqrt{3}$)/2 | B.) ( -9$\pm\sqrt{97}$ /2 | C.) ( -2 $\pm\sqrt{10}$)/2 | D.) X =0 , X = 3 | E.) ( 1 $\pm$ i$\sqrt{5}$) /3 |
| F.) (-4$\pm\sqrt{10}$)/6 | G.) -4$\pm\sqrt{14}$ | H.) (3$\pm$i$\sqrt{23}$) /8 | I.) X=3,X=-3 | J.) $\pm$i$\sqrt{3}$ |
| K.) (4$\pm\sqrt{20.8}$)/2.4 | L.) $\pm$ 2$\sqrt{3}$ | M.) $\pm\sqrt{2}$ / 2 | N.) X =0 ,X =2 | O.) X = 0,X =-6 |
| P.) X =0,X =-32 | Q.) (3$\pm$i$\sqrt{87}$)/8 | R.) X =1/2, X =0 | S.) $\pm$5 | |

# Quadratic Equations 4

| First rectangle | No | No | | Second rectangle | Yes | | Third Rectangle | No | No |
|---|---|---|---|---|---|---|---|---|---|
| | Yes | No | | | No | | | Yes | Yes |
| | No | Yes | | | Yes | | | No | |
| | | | | | Yes | | | No | |
| | | | | | No | | | | |
| | | | | | Yes | | | | |

### Divisibility Rules 1

N,Y,N,N,N,N,N,N,N,

NN,N,Y,N,N,N,N,N

N,Y,N,N,N,N,N,N,N

Y,Y,N,Y,Y,N,Y,Y,N

Y,N,N,N,N,N,N,N,N,

Y,Y,Y,N,Y,Y,Y,N,Y

Y,Y,N,N,Y,N,Y,N,Y

---

### Square Roots

The square root of a number is determined by using prime factors.

A.) $\sqrt{4} = \sqrt{(2)(2)} = 2$          B.) $\sqrt{36} = \sqrt{(2)(3)(2)(3)} = \sqrt{(2)(3)} = 6$          C.) $\sqrt{8} = \sqrt{(2)(2)(2)} = 2\sqrt{2}$

D.) $\sqrt{32} = \sqrt{(2)(2)(2)(2)(2)} = (2)(2)\sqrt{2} = 4\sqrt{2}$          E.) $\sqrt{24a^2b^2c^2} = \sqrt{(2)(2)(2)(3)aabbcc} = 2abc\sqrt{6}$

F.) $\sqrt{40a^3b^6c^5} = \sqrt{(2)(2)(2)(5)aaabbbbbbccccc} = 2ab^2c^2\sqrt{10ac}$

A square root cannot be in the denominator.

A.) $\sqrt{2}/\sqrt{3} = \sqrt{2}/\sqrt{3}(\sqrt{3}/\sqrt{3}) = \sqrt{6}/\sqrt{9} = \sqrt{6}/3$   B. $(1/\sqrt{3})(\sqrt{3}/\sqrt{3}) = \sqrt{3}/\sqrt{9} = \sqrt{3}/3$

When adding square roots, the square root most of the time should be the same square root in the given parts.

1. $\sqrt{20} + \sqrt{180} = \sqrt{(2)(2)(5)} + \sqrt{(2)(3)(3)(5)(2)} = 2\sqrt{5} + (2)(3)\sqrt{5} = 2\sqrt{5} + 6\sqrt{5} = 8\sqrt{5}$

2. $\sqrt{32b^5} - \sqrt{18ab^3} = \sqrt{(2)(2)(2)(2)(2)bbbbb} - \sqrt{(3)(3)(2)abbb} = 4b^2\sqrt{2b} - 3b\sqrt{2b} = \sqrt{2b}(4b^2 - 3b)$

The student should learn the divisibility rules.

# Multiplying Square Roots Example

$$(\sqrt{8} - 4)(\sqrt{2} + \sqrt{5}) = \sqrt{16} + \sqrt{40} \quad -4\sqrt{2} - 4\sqrt{5}$$
$$= 4 + \sqrt{(4)(2)(5)} -4\sqrt{2} -4\sqrt{5}$$
$$4 + 2\sqrt{10} -4\sqrt{2} -4\sqrt{5}$$

## Perfect Square Roots 2

A. 2      B. 3      C. 11      D. 22      E. 6      F. 16      G. 40      H. 10      I. 21      J. 5
K. 20     L. 9      M. 13      N. 4      O. 35      P.18      Q. 8      R. 14      S. 17      T. 7
U. 25

## Square Roots 3

1). $2\sqrt{2}$      2.) $3\sqrt{2}$      3.) $2\sqrt{3}$      4.) $2\sqrt{5}$      5). $2\sqrt{7}$      6.) $6\sqrt{2}$      7.) $5\sqrt{3}$      8.) $2\sqrt{11}$      9.) $4\sqrt{3}$

10.) $10\sqrt{2}$  11.) $2\sqrt{21}$  12.) $2\sqrt{35}$  13.) $2\sqrt{14}$  14.) $\sqrt{21}$  15.) $5\sqrt{6}$  16. $2\sqrt{23}$  17.) $3\sqrt{14}$  18.) $4\sqrt{5}$

19.) $\sqrt{2}$      20.) $3\sqrt{3}$      21.) $10\sqrt{3}$   Jack ,Red , and Mary

## Square Roots 4

1.) $2a^3b^4c\sqrt{b}$          2.) $2ab2c3$          3.) $3ac^2\sqrt{3ac}$          4.) $5a\sqrt{a}$          5.) $3ab^3c^4\sqrt{2b}$
6.) $2b^2c^3\sqrt{2abc}$      7.) $4a^3b^4\sqrt{5ab}$      8.) $8a^4b^4c^3\sqrt{ac}$      9.) $2ab^3c^4d^4\sqrt{30abc}$  10.) $12ab^3\sqrt{2a}$
11.) $10a^2\sqrt{10a}$      12.) $5a^3b^2c^{18}\sqrt{10ab}$  13.) $2a^6b^6c^{27}\sqrt{21b}$  14.) $20c^4\sqrt{abc}$      15.) $9ac^2\sqrt{b}$

## Square Roots 5

1.) $\sqrt{28}$ F K Q      2.) $\sqrt{200}$ G I Z      3.) $\sqrt{18}$ A O U      4.) $\sqrt{98}$ E P R      5.) $\sqrt{360}$ H J S
6.) $\sqrt{1000}$ C ,L,T      7.) $\sqrt{8}$ D,N,B

## Square Roots 6

| 11 | 10 |
|----|----|
| 7  | 7  |

## Rationalizing the Denominator 7

1) M          2) F          3) I          4) E          5) J          6) P          7) G
8) C          9) A          10) L          11) B          12) D          13) H          14) Q

# Square Roots 8

Team B is greater

# Square Roots 9

A.) -1√5     B.) 2√5     C.) 6√3     D.) 5√2          E.) 10√10     F.) 5√2 + 2√3     G.) -2√2 -2√7     H.) 5√3

I.) √5       J.) 21       K.) -√15     L.) √3 + 4√5     M.) 11√2      N.) 12√2 -4√3     O.) 72          Q.) 10√3

# Square Roots 10

Black -6 , ( 12√2 + 4√6 -4√30 -4√10)          Blue 6 , (2 √3 + 4 √2 ) , -16√3, 12

Red ( 2√2 +6 -√6 - 3√3 ) ,10√2+5√6+6√3          Gray -2

Green (4 + 2√3 -2√2 -√6 )                        Yellow 12

Orange ( 9 + 3√5 -√15 -3√3 )                     Purple 1

# Radical Equations 11

1.) 4.5        2.) 162       3.) 108       4.) 18        5.) 40.5        6.) 18

7.) 39         8.) 260       9.) .024      10.) 5.8      11.) (-6,3)     12.) .85 ,-2.35

# Radical Equations 12

12 and 7 Red 8     2 Red  200  3 Red  1/18     8 Red  128     6 Yellow  100   9 Yellow  4.5

1 Yellow  8.23 and-.25   5 Yellow  (8± 2√7)/2  10 Green  24   4 Green (9 ±√17)/2

11 Green  2.62 and .38

# Pythagorean Theorem

$$a^2 + b^2 = c^2$$

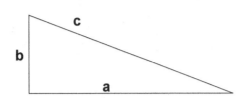

$a = 2$ , $b = 3$ , Find $c = ?$     $a^2 + b^2 = c^2$     2. $a = 8$ , $c = 12 =$ , Find $b$ ?

$$2^2 + 3^2 = c^2 \qquad\qquad a^2 + b^2 = c^2$$
$$4 + 9 = c^2 \qquad\qquad 8^2 + b^2 = 12^2$$
$$13 = c^2 \qquad\qquad 64 + b^2 = 144$$
$$\sqrt{13} = c \qquad\qquad -64 \quad = -64$$
$$b^2 = 80$$
$$b = \sqrt{80} = 4\sqrt{5}$$

## Pythagorean Theorem 1

Find HS = 3.6 , SB = 15.6 , BU = 12.10 , UE = 21.10 , EG = 13.7 , GK = 36.62 , KH = 4

## Pythagorean Theorem 2

Find $C_1$= 1.73 , $C_2$= 2 , $C_3$ = 4.48 , $C_4$= 7.48 , $C_5$= 11.70 , $C_6$ = 17.49 , $C_7$ = 23.04 , $C_8$ = 31.86
    $C_9$ = 45.16 , $C_{10}$ = 57.13 , $C_{11}$ = 63.62

## Pythagorean Theorem 3

1.) 2.24     2.) 4.48     3.) 6.72     4.) 8.96     5.) 11.20     6.) 13.     7.) 15.68

### Polynomial

Add two polynomials    $4X^3 + 2X^2 - 4X + 6$     Subtract    $X^6 + 6X^4 - 3X^2 - X + 8$ from

$$\underline{-7X^3 - 3X^2 + 3X - 7} \qquad\qquad -X^5 + X^4 - 3X^2 - 3X + 3$$
$$-3X^3 - 1X^2 - 1X - 1$$

Answer    $(-X^5 + X^4 - 3X + 3)$

$$\underline{-X^6 - 6X^4 + 3X^2 + 1X - 8\ )}$$
$$-X^6 - X^5 - 5X^4 + 3X^2 - 2X - 5$$

# Polynomials 1

1.) A + B  2.) A + C  3.) C + B  4.) C – A  5.) A - C
6.) B - C  7.) C - B  8.) B -A  9.) A – A  10.) A - B
11.) $-x^3+ 4x^2 – 9x -2$  12.) $X^3-2x^2+ x + 1$  13.) $X^2-2x + 6$  14.) $X^3-2x^2+ 5x + 14$

# Polynomials 2

$-(X^3 - X^2 + 2X – 2) -( X^2 + 3X -3 ) -( 3X^3 + 2X – 3) - (-4 X^3 –X^2 +3X + 14 )-(X^3+3X^2 -18X - 7)$

$-(-4X^2 + 3X + 1 ) -(2X^2 -4X - 5 )= X^2 +7X + 11$

# Polynomials 3

1. $3X,X,X,3X (4X)$  2. $4X^2-X + 5, 4X^2-X + 3, X^2 -3X, X^2 -3X +2 (5x^2-4X + 5)$
3. $3X^2 -6X + 6 ,X^3 +2X^2 -2x + 2, 2x^3-2x^2 +x – 6 , x^3 –x^2-3x-2, (2x^3 + x^2-5x)$

# Polynomials 4

$4X^5 + 2X^3 + 2X^2 + X$    $X^6-3X^4+5X^3+ X^2-3X -14$    $X^9 + X^5 +X^4-X^3-36X + 23$

# Polynomials 5

$-2X^2 -4X + 16$    $X^2 -4X +9$   $-3X^2 -7X + 12$    $= -6X + 18$

# Ordered Pairs 1

A (-2,5)  B (-3,7)  C (-3,9)  D (-2 ,11)  E (0,11)  Y (4,0)  G (1, 7)  R (-3 ,-11)
K (0 , 3)  L (4,-2)  M (5,-4)  N (3 ,-8)  O (2,-5)  P (1,-2)  Q (1,-11)  T (-5,-2)
X (-4,0)

# Ordered Pairs 2

A (3,0)  B (1 ,-1)  C (0 ,3)  D (-1 ,1)  E (-3,7.6)  F (-1 ,-1)  G (0 ,-3)  H (1 ,-1)
I (3 ,0)  J (9,0)  K (9.4 ,4)  L (0,4)  M (-3.5, 4)  N (-9,0)  O (-3,-4)  P (0 ,6)

## Ordered Pairs 3

Hammer

## Ordered Pairs 4

A (2, -6)    B (-2, -6.5)  C (6, 6)    D (9, -6)    E (2, -.5)    F (-10.5, -4.5 )   G (-4/5, -2)  H (-6, 6)

## Distance Formula

$$( X_1 , Y_1 )         ( X_2 , Y_2 )$$

$$D = (\sqrt{ (X_2 -X_1)^2 + (Y_2 - Y_1)^2}$$     Use ( 4, 7 )    and    ( -4 , 5 )

$$D = (\sqrt{(-4 - 4)^2 + (5 - 7)^2} = \sqrt{-8^2 + -2^2} = \sqrt{64 + 4} = \sqrt{68} = 8.25$$

## Distance Formulas 1

Yes or No        73.1

## Distance Formulas 2

Yes or No        6.7+4.1 + 5.8 + 5 + 4.1 + 8.1 +8.1 = 41.9

## Slope of a Line

M = Y / X or 15/5 = 3 /1        M = Y /X or -15/ 5 = -3 / 1        M = Y / X or 0/123 =        M = Y / X or
67 / `0 = undefined

## Slope of a Line 1

1. AB = 5/1      2. BC = undefined   3. CD = 2/3       4. DE = -5/2      5. EF = undefined
6. = 0        7. GH = 7/2      8. HJ = 5/11       9. JK = 45/17       10. LK= 0
11. MN = -12/3

# Slopes of Lines 2

1. 5/3          2. -3/4          3. -7 /3          4. 0/3 = 0     5. 0          6. 0          7. 3/2          8. -2/5
9. -2/1          10. 5/6          11. -9/2          12. 5 /3          13. 5/2          14. 0          15. -4/5          16. 5/9
17. undefined                    18. -1/2          19. 5/3          20. −3/ 3     21. -7/2          22. Undefined
23. 5 /3          24. -9/2 24 -5 / 2.5

# Slopes of Lines 3

Many answers

# Slopes of Lines 4

1.Red .20 ,-.50 , -.33                    Yellow 2 , -.57          Blue -.25 .125                    Green 0 1 , 1

Orange undefined , -1.75          Brown = 6, 4          Black 0 ,.67

# Slope of Lines 5

-3 , 6 , 1 , -1 , -1/2 , 6          -2/3 , 2/3 , undefined , 0 , -9/5          5/6 , -8/3 , -5/4 , 1/3

# Find the slopes and y-intercept

Y =Mx + b                    M= the slope,                    Y-intercept = b

1/3X + 2/4Y = 2                    12(1/3X + 2/4 Y = 2 )                    4X + 6Y = 24

6Y = -4X + 24          Y = -4X/6 + 4                    M = -2/3,                    b = 4

## Slopes and Y-intercept 6

Orange M = 2 , b= 3      Green M = 3 /4 , b = -1      Blue M = -2 , b= 7

Yellow M = 3 , b = -4      Purple M = undefined , b = none      White M =0 , b = 6

Brown M = -3/2 , b = 3      Red M = -3 , b = 18      Tan  M=0  b= 6

## Equations of Lines 7

1. B     2. Z     3. C     4. G     5. A     6. D     7. F     8. T     9. E     10. H     11. I

## Equations of lines 8

Kite and four triangles

## Equations of Lines 9

Equations 4, 10, and 13

## Equations of Lines 10

A     I     J     B     G     C     F     E     D     H

# Equations of Lines 11

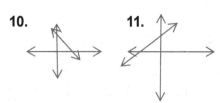

1.  2.  3.  4.  5.  6.  7.  8.  9.

10.  11.

## Linear Equations

All equations accepts 1/xy =17     (x + Y ) /Y     xy=4     x/y=y/x ,y=X²,X =y²,

**X – X/y – 2, y = I X + 3I, 2Y² = X² ,y = 1/2X² ,Y - 2X + √2.**

## Linear Equations 2

A is a box                     B is a kite                     C is an Octagon

## Equations and Graphs 1

1. M = -3/4          y = -3/4x + 3   (0,3) (4 , 0)     x= 0 , 4 , -4 , 8
                                                        Y = 3 , 0 , 6 , -3

2. M= undefined   x = 0          (3 ,0) None     x = 0 , 0 , 0 , 0
                                                        Y = 1 ,-6 , 1 , -2

3. M = 0            y = 0          None (0 , 4)   x= 1 , 3 ,-3 ,4
                                                        Y = 0 , 0 , 0 , 0

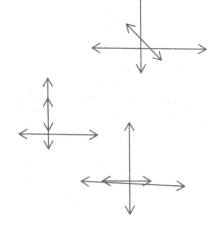

# Equations and Graphs 2

1. M = -1 /2    y = -1/2x + 4    (0, 4)(8 , 0)        x = 0 , 2 , 4 , -4
                                                       Y = 4 , 3 , 2 , 6

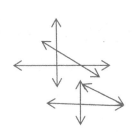

2. M= -1      y = -x + 13     (0 , 13) (13 , 0)        x = 0 , 1 , 2 , -1
                                                       Y = 13 , 12, 11, 14

3. M = 22     66x -3y = 35   ( 0 , -11 2/3) )(35/66, 0)  x = 0 , 35/66
                                                         Y =-11 2/3, 0

# Zeros of the Functions 1

F(x) = 6x + 5 Let F(x) = 0,find x        6x + 5 = 0
                                         -5 = -5
                                         6x = -5
                                         X = -5/6

| | | | | |
|---|---|---|---|---|
| 1. Green 1.5 | 2. Gray -1 | 3. Blue -1/5 | 4. Yellow 0 | 5. Orange -10.5 |
| 6. Red ½ | 7. Brown 1 | 8. Black 5 | 9. Red 5 | 10. Pink -3 |
| 11. Purple -12 | 12. White No solution | 13. Tan -2 1/3 | 14. Pink (1 ,-2) | |

# Systems of Lines

| Crossing | Parallel | Following | Perpendicular |
|---|---|---|---|
| $M_1 \# M_2$ | $M_1 = M_2$ | $M_1 = M_2$ | $(M_1)(M_2) = -1$ |
| $B_1 \# B_2$ | $B_1 \# B_2$ | $B_1 = B_2$ | $B_1 \# B_2$ |

# Systems of Equations 1

| Consistent Independent | Inconsistent | Consistent Dependent | Consistent Independent |
|---|---|---|---|
| Crossing | Parallels | Same Lines | Perpendicular lines |
| A   and   J | A   and   F | A   and   E | C   and   G |
| A   and   C | A   and   H | | |
| E   and   I | E   and   F | | |
| F   and   I | F   and   H | | |
| A   and   I | B   and   J | | |

# Systems of Equations 2

**Solve by using the Substitution Method**

| | |
|---|---|
| 2X + 3Y =6 | X - Y = 4 |
| 2X + 3Y = 6 | Y = + Y |
| 2(4+ Y) + 3Y = 6 | X = 4 + Y |
| 8 + 2Y + 3Y = 6 | X = 4 + -2 /5 |
| 8 + 5Y = 6 | X = 3 3/5 |
| -8 = -8 | |
| 5Y = -2 | |
| Y = -2 /5 | ( 3 3/5 , -2 /5 ) |

1. (-3,5/2)     2. (10/3 ,-2/3)    3. (-7 1/5 , 3/5)   4. (32/5 ,-8/5)    5. (8/5 , -12/5)    6. (-48/11,30/11)

7. (12,-24)     8. ( ¼ , -87/4 )    9. (10/3 , -2/3)

## Solving Equations for X and Y 3

| 1. | 2. | 3. | 4. | 5. | 6. | 7. | 8. | 9. | 10. | 11. |
|---|---|---|---|---|---|---|---|---|---|---|
| X =4 | -2 | 6 | 2 4/7 | -2/15 | 4 | 0 | NA | 1 3/4 | 0 | 1 1/5 |
| Y=-2/3 | -7 | -1 | 1 1/7 | 1 1/15 | 0 | -3 | NA | 1 /2 | 6 | 18/5 |

## Systems of Equations 4

Many solutions

## Functions or Not a Function

**Use a vertical line to determine the function. The vertical line will touch the graph at one point if a function exists.**

| **Function or Not a Function 1** | | | | **Function or Not a Function 2** | | | | |
|---|---|---|---|---|---|---|---|---|
| Yes | Yes | No | Yes | No | Yes | Yes | Yes | Yes |
| No | Yes | No | No | Yes | No | Yes | No | Yes |
| Yes | Yes | Yes | No | Yes | No | Yes | Yes | Yes |
| Yes | Yes | No | Yes | No | No | No | No | No |

# Variations

## Direct Variations
If y is 12 when x is 2, find y when x is 6

| | |
|---|---|
| $Y = Kx$ | $Y = Kx$ |
| $12 = K(2)$ | $Y = (6)(6)$ |
| $6 = K$ | $Y = 36$ |

## Inverse Variations
If y is 20 when x is 4, find y when x is 6

| | |
|---|---|
| $Y = K / x$ | $Y = K / x$ |
| $20 = K / 4$ | $Y = 80 / 6$ |
| $(4)(20) = (K / 4)(4)$ | $Y = 13\ 1/3$ |
| $80 = K$ | |

## Direct and Inverse Variations as the Square of x
If y is 20 when u is 3, v is 5 and s is 2, find Y when u is 3, v is 2 and s is 3

| | |
|---|---|
| $Y = KUV / S^2$ | $Y = KUV / S^2$ |
| $20 = K(3)(5) / 2^2$ | $Y = (16/3\ )(3)(2)/3^2$ |
| $20 = 15K / 4$ | $Y = 3\ 5/9$ |
| $(4)(20) = 15K / 4\ (4)$ | |
| $80 = 15K$ | |
| $80/15 = 15K / 15$ | |
| $5\ 1/3 = K$ | |

## Direct Variations as the Square of x
If y is 40 when x is 2, find Y when x is 2

| | |
|---|---|
| $Y = K x^2$ | $Y = K x^2$ |
| $40 = K(2)^2$ | $Y = (10)(2^2)$ |
| $40 = 4K$ | $Y = 40$ |
| $40/4\ 4K/4$ | |
| $10 = K$ | |

## Variations 1

| Direct Variations | Inverse Variations | Direct and inverse variation as the square of s |
|---|---|---|
| 1. K = 6, y = 12 | 1. K = 80 , Y = 20 | 1. K = 16/3 , 3 5/9 |
| 2. K = 2 , y = 12 | 2. K = 30, Y = 7.5 | 2. K = 16/3 y = 8/3 |
| 3. K = 1/10 , y = 3 | 3. K = -40 , Y = -6 2/3 | |
| 4. K = 1/10 , y = 2/5 | 4. K = 600, Y = 100 | |

# Direct Variations as the square of x

1. K = 10 , y = 40
2. K = 10/3 , y = 5/6

## Matrices 1

| 1. | 3 | 6 | | 2. | 1 | 1 | | 3. | 0 | -6 | | 4. | -1 | 0 | | 5. | 0 | -2 | | 6. | 0 | 1 |
|----|---|---|---|----|---|---|---|----|---|----|---|----|----|---|---|----|---|----|---|----|---|---|
| | 10 | 14 | | | 2 | 3 | | | 2 | -2 | | | 0 | 0 | | | -3 | -3 | | | 2 | 3 |

| 7. | 5 | 12 | | 8. | 1/2 | 3/2 | | 9. | -.5 | -1.5 | | 10. | 12 | 20 | | 11. | 14 | -33 |
|----|---|----|---|----|-----|-----|---|----|------|------|---|-----|----|----|---|-----|----|-----|
| | 19 | 26 | | | 5/2 | 7/2 | | | -2.5 | -3.5 | | | 32 | 44 | | | -46 | -50 |

| 12. | 2/3 | -8/3 | | 13. | ½ | 4.5 | | 14. | 1.5 | 2.4 | | 15. | 5 | 13 | | 16. | 2.8 | 1.2 |
|-----|-----|------|---|-----|---|-----|---|-----|-----|-----|---|-----|---|----|---|-----|-----|-----|
| | 10/3 | -4/3 | | | 1.5 | 4.5 | | | 3.9 | 5.4 | | | 21 | 29 | | | 2.0 | 4.8 |

## Matrices 2

| 35 | -- | -- | -- | -- | -- | -- | 39 | 19 , 20 |
|----|----|----|----|----|----|----|----|---------|
| 29 | 23 | -- | 1 | 2 | 7 | 11 | ------- | |
| 31 | --- | --- | --- | 26 | 3 | 17 | 25 | |
| 32 | --- | 5,18 | 24 | 40 | --- | --- | -- | |
| 33 | --- | 9 | --- | --- | --- | 14 | --- | |
| 8 | 13 | 12 | --- | 38 | 27 | --- | --- | |
| --- | --- | ---- | --- | 34 | 30 | 10 | --- | |
| 28 | 36 | 15,16 | 4 | 37 | --- | 6 | 21,22 | |

## Matrices 3

| 1. Ball | 2. Shoes | 3. Box | 4. Box | 5. Ring | 6. Bike | 7. Car |
|---------|----------|--------|--------|---------|---------|--------|
| 8. Truck | 9. Ring | 9a. Hat | 10. Girls Face | 11. Kite | 12. Boat | 13. Pin |
| 14. Comb | 15. Ball | 16. Comb | 17. Boy | 18. Ring | 19.Girl's Face | 20. Boy |
| 21. Pin | 22. Girl's Face | 23. Eight | 24. Bike | 25. Boat | 26. Ring | |

# Mode

MATHEMATICS   CAN   BE   FUN.

# Median

(28 + 62 + 50.5) = 140.5          (92.5+43.0 + 14.5 = 150          (5 + 5.50 +4.5) = 15.0
(3 +2.5 + 2) = 7.5               (2.5 + 3) = 5.5

# Averages

| | | | | | | | |
|---|---|---|---|---|---|---|---|
| 1. -4.2 | 2. -5.49 | 3. -4.49 | 4. .74 | 5. -187 | 6. 2.6 | 7. 6.0 | 8. 31.65 |
| 9. -5.5 | 10. 493.8 | 11. 1.5 | 12. 22.90 | 13. -23.3 | 14. .80 | 15. -17.50 | 16. 313.50 |
| 17. 3.8 | 18. 1.88 | 19. 5.21 | 20. 34.93 | 21. -35.93 | 22. -1.2 | 23. -.7 | 24. 1.2 |
| 25. 3.3 | | | | | | | |

# Mode   Median   Mean

1. 3 , 10 , 8.5    2. 255          3. 4.5          4. single          5. Median          6. Mode values

7. The mean is affected by the extreme values, where median is not. Mode is affected by the amount of repetition of values

8. Mode is the number that occur the most in a set of data.

Median is the number in the middle of a group of data in the correct order from the smallest to largest.

Average is the sum of the numbers divided by the number of elements in the set.

# Box and Whisker Plots

1. No median, No scale of numbers   2. No median, No maximum point, No scale   3. No minimum point, No median, No scale   4. No minimum point, No median, No maximum point, No scale,   5. No lower quartile, No median, No upper quartile, No scale   6. No  lower quartile, No third quartile, No scale
7. No median   8. 100 – 10 = 90   9. 55   10. Not given.

# Percentages 1

45% = # 5  ,  30% = # 8  ,  133.3% = # 10  ,  500% = # 9  ,  75% = # 1  ,  62.5% = # 2

166% = # 4  ,  8% = # 7  ,  115.5% = # 3  ,  90% = # 6

# Percentages 2

| 320 L | | 300 T | | 250 I |
|---|---|---|---|---|
| | 17.5 G | | 1080 K | |
| 45 W | | 27 A | | 92C |
| | 249.75 E | | 160 J | |
| 2837.14 H | | 2500 F | | 3.92B |
| | 16.67 S | | 166.7 D | |
| | | | | |

# Circle 1

1. 100      2. Beth 20%, George 50%, Sam 20%, Dennis 10%      3. None      4. 25

5. Number of Students in a class    6. 20    7. 20    8. 5/1    9. 1/1    10. 1/2    11. 1 to 1

12. 1.50      13. .60      14. 40